ALTERNATION

ALTERNATION

Transform. Embellish. Customize.

Shannon Okey + Alexandra Underhill

NORTH LIGHT BOOKS
Cincinnati, Ohio

11   10   09   08   07   5   4   3   2   1

Library of Congress Cataloging-in-Publication Data

Okey, Shannon, 1975-
  AlterNation / Shannon Okey and Alexandra Underhill.
     p. cm.
  Includes bibliographical references and index.
  ISBN 978-1-58180-978-7 (alk. paper)
  1. Machine sewing. 2. Tailoring. 3. Clothing and dress. I. Underhill, Alexandra. II. Title.
TT713.O385 2007
646.2'044--dc22

2006102320

Distributed in Canada by Fraser Direct
100 Armstrong Avenue
Georgetown, ON, Canada L7G 5S4
Tel: (905) 877-4411

Distributed in the U.K. and Europe by
David & Charles
Brunel House, Newton Abbot, Devon,
TQ12 4PU, England
Tel: (+44) 1626 323200,
Fax: (+44) 1626 323319
E-mail: postmaster@davidandcharles.co.uk

Distributed in Australia by Capricorn Link
P.O. Box 704, South Windsor,
NSW 2756 Australia
Tel: (02) 4577-3555

METRIC CONVERSION CHART

TO CONVERT	TO	MULTIPLY BY
Inches	Centimeters	2.54
Centimeters	Inches	0.4
Feet	Centimeters	30.5
Centimeters	Feet	0.03
Yards	Meters	0.9
Meters	Yards	1.1
Sq. Inches	Sq. Centimeters	6.45
Sq. Centimeters	Sq. Inches	0.16
Sq. Feet	Sq. Meters	0.09
Sq. Meters	Sq. Feet	10.8
Sq. Yards	Sq. Meters	0.8
Sq. Meters	Sq. Yards	1.2
Pounds	Kilograms	0.45
Kilograms	Pounds	2.2
Ounces	Grams	28.3
Grams	Ounces	0.035

fw
F+W PUBLICATIONS, INC.
www.fwbookstore.com

Model Photography: Slade Photography,
        sladephotography.com
Stylist: Dina Amsden
All Other Photography: Christine Okey

ACKNOWLEDGMENTS

Alexandra and Shannon would both like to thank Slade Photography in Los Angeles and Christine Okey in Cleveland for brilliant model and how-to shots, respectively, and all the thrift stores of greater Cleveland that yield riches for us on a regular basis. The model photography knocked both of us out of our chairs … and those were just the test shots! Additional, extra-special thanks to model Samantha Grace for helping us work out the initial shots.

Thanks to Sarah Patterson for assisting at the photo shoots and pinch-hitting as a model when time was tight. (Thanks to all our friends, friends' friends and neighbors who got drafted into modeling, for that matter.) Sarah actually designed the only piece in the book not sewn by either of us (*Pieced Pants*); we handed her a stack of stuff during a shoot and said: "Here you go, see what you can make with these." She's an exemplary stitcher, a designer in her own right, and you'll no doubt be seeing her name in more places soon. Megan Engelmann took over some of Shannon's sewing duties during the editing phase of the book, which made a big difference in getting things done. Arabella Proffer Vendetta drew the amazing illustrations, painted the cowboy boots and modeled, too. She's multi-multitalented, just like Christine Okey (Shannon's mom), who painted the suit jacket and helped stitch a few things together when she wasn't doing the photography.

Tamas Jakab? Well, he gets love from both of us for helping edit and format the how-to shots, but superspecial thanks from Shannon for being the best boyfriend in the world, and taking over many household duties during Heavy Writing and Heavy Editing modes.

The rest of our extended networks of friends and family also offered their love and support, which is appreciated more than they will ever know.

ABOUT THE AUTHORS

Just who are we, anyway? We're Alexandra (Xan) Underhill and Shannon Okey.

Xan (top right) is an ultratalented sculptor in all mediums, including fabric. She's done costuming for many productions you've heard of (like Cirque du Soleil) and some that you haven't … yet. She's best known for her tie skirts (the pattern's on page 92 if you want to make your own), which she demo'ed on crafty TV show *Uncommon Threads,* and her stilt dancing. Xan teaches art workshops in residencies all over the place, has a fabric stash to die for, and is a regular at Burning Man. This is her first book.

Shannon (bottom right) is a fiber fanatic who knits, spins, crochets, dyes, felts and much more. She's got multiple spinning wheels, knitting machines and looms, as well as fiber by the pound in her studio. Shannon's best known for her *Knitgrrl* books and several other crafty titles (see The Guide, page 140). She has appeared on *Uncommon Threads, Knitty Gritty* and *Crafters Coast to Coast,* coordinates the Cleveland edition of indie craft fair Bazaar Bizarre, is a columnist for *knit.1* magazine and is a frequent contributor to magazines such as *CRAFT, Adorn* and *Yarn Market Knitting News.*

Together, we've worked on a number of projects, such as a touch-sensitive fabric iPod wedding dress called "iDo" for the computational couture show Seamless, and of course, this book. Our goal for *AlterNation* is to inspire you, to teach techniques you can apply to your own projects and encourage you to share the love.

With that, we invite you to continue the crafty dialogue at www.alternationbook.com. It's like a twenty-four-hour party with glue guns and sergers instead of cocktails and canapés.

CONTENTS

INTRODUCTION

Do-it-yourself fashion is the only reliable way to avoid looking like a mall store exploded in your closet. Whether you can't pick up a needle without spilling blood or can operate a sewing machine in your sleep, this book will give you tips, tricks and project ideas to create your own unique styles with maximum impact and minimal cost.

Does threading a sewing machine give you the chills? Fear not! Some projects in this book can be made with nothing but an iron! Wherever possible, we'll give you multiple options that will appeal to both new and advanced stitchers.

The concept behind *AlterNation* is literally in the title—we'd like to see everyone, coast to coast, daring to be different by revamping clothes in their own style. No more cookie-cutter catalog dictators telling you what to wear. No more buying everything off the rack. No more spending two hundred dollars on a pair of the latest "it" jeans when you can make something two hundred times cooler for five dollars and a little sewing time.

Reduce, reuse, recycle—it's not just a slogan, it's a way of life. Our grandmothers knew this well, although for them it was based more on necessity than enviro-chic. Not only did they drop and raise hemlines regularly to keep their skirts at This Year's Fashionable Length, but they also reused precious fabric in unusual ways. Believe us, the *Denim Ballgown Skirt* on page 98 is not the first time a pair of men's pants has been made into a skirt—and if you've ever seen the Quilts of Gee's Bend exhibit or book, you know that lowly denim work pants can become a spectacular work of art in the hands of a crafty woman.

For those of you who are more trend-focused than crunchy granola recycle-mama, though, keep this in mind: When you make your own clothes, they're truly one of a kind. No worries about showing up to a party or event wearing the same outfit as four other people. And if someone asks you where you got it, just say it was custom made for you!

Set the trends, don't follow them: That's our operating principle.

So, if you want unique fashion that's easy to make and doesn't cost a lot, you'll love *AlterNation*. Don't worry if you can't find the exact same materials we used in a pattern. Digging through the back of your closet, attic or the local thrift store will yield different stuff. Consider it a challenge to apply the techniques you learn here. And don't forget about our Web site: www.alternationbook.com. We'd love to see what you come up with!

THE SEWING KIT: TOOLS AND TECHNIQUES

The top three skills you will need for most projects in this book are:

- using a needle (or sewing machine) to sew a relatively straight line
- cutting fabric with sharp scissors or a rotary cutter
- ironing cloth with a hot iron

That's it! Detailed information on specialized techniques or equipment such as grommet tools and ink-jet printers will be presented alongside the projects that use them. We're going to run down the basics of sewing, cutting and ironing here; even if you're an experienced seamstress, you might want to give it a glance. We're fond of some unconventional materials and techniques. For example, masking tape is to sewing what duct tape is to the rest of the universe: Just when you think it can't possibly do what you need, it surprises you.

HAND SEWING: THE BASICS

Never sewn by hand before? To get started, all you need is a needle, thread, and some pins to hold things together while you work.

Needles and Pins

Different needles have different purposes. Needles meant for embroidery thread have larger eyes; if you're sewing a delicate fabric, you'll use a thinner needle than you would for a heavy winter coat. When in doubt, ask your local fabric store or a friend who sews which needle would work best on the fabric you want to use, or buy multipurpose needle packs and experiment.

Any type of straight pins will work for the projects in this book. Safety pins can be helpful, too.

Thread

Although there are some specialized types of thread designed for particular types of projects, most sewing thread is 100 percent cotton, polyester or a cotton/polyester blend (the polyester adds strength). It comes in a wide range of colors to match almost any color fabric you might want to sew. Chances are you'll be set for most projects if you have both black and white thread plus a few neutral colors like gray, brown and denim blue. If you're sewing something that contains multiple colors, choose a thread that will match the largest section of the right side of the fabric best.

To get started, cut a length of thread. Anything over a yard (1 meter) tangles too easily to be practical; 12–18 inches (30–46cm) works best. Hold the cut tip to the eye of your needle, push it into the eye, and pull a third of the thread's length through to the other side. If the end of your thread is a little frayed, your scissors may need sharpening. This is why some sewers put the end of their thread in their mouth—the moisture temporarily "glues" the fibers together and gets it through the needle smoothly. Cutting the tip of the thread at an angle also helps. Don't forget to make a small knot at the end of the long side to anchor your stitches.

THE STRAIGHT STITCH

In its simplest form, a line of straight sewing looks like a series of dashes. The stitches on top of the fabric have spaces between them where the needle has gone underneath. You can keep both upper and lower stitches the same size or make them slightly different. When hemming a skirt, for example, the stitches on the public side of the fabric are usually quite a bit smaller than the stitches running behind. When in doubt, aim for consistency and even stitch size.

Hand sewers have an advantage over machine sewers that can sometimes compensate for lack of speed: they can make their stitches any size they want. When you sew by hand, the sky is the limit, from teensy tiny invisible stitches to great big rough basting stitches. (Basting is temporary stitching to hold two pieces together while you do something else.)

STEP 1 | PUSH NEEDLE THROUGH FABRIC "ZIGZAG"

Instead of sewing each stitch individually by putting the needle up through the fabric, pulling out all the thread, then putting it back down through the fabric, you can push the fabric onto your needle 1" (3cm) or so at a time. Push the needle through the fabric on alternate sides several times in a row (being careful to keep your stitches even), and move the fabric back onto the needle as you go. Now push the needle through the fabric "zigzag" with your dominant hand.

STEP 2 | PULL THREAD THROUGH

Complete pulling the needle and its accompanying thread through with your nondominant hand.

Keeping Straight Stitches Even

The most difficult part of sewing can be keeping your stitches even. Here's a trick to make hand sewing in a straight line easy: Use tailor's chalk or masking tape to mark the place you want to sew. From there, it's just a question of connecting the lines with dashes. And no, we're not kidding about the masking tape. If you have a tough time keeping your lines straight, and the fabric you're sewing isn't furry or otherwise in danger of coming off on the tape (test in a small area first if you're concerned), you can apply the tape on one side of the pieces you're sewing together and stitch along its edge. Should you sew through the tape, you can rip it out without harming your stitches.

THE WHIPSTITCH

To whipstitch (also called the overcast stitch), push the needle from the back of the fabric to the front. Take it back over the edge of the fabric, bringing the needle from the back through the front again. This is frequently used as a temporary (basting) stitch along an edge, or to close an opening that is too small or too tricky to fit through a sewing machine (for example, installing a zipper in an unusual place).

STEP 1 | INSERT NEEDLE FROM BACK TO FRONT

Place the needle through the fabric back to front along the edge.

STEP 2 | PULL THREAD THROUGH

Pull the needle and its accompanying thread through. The next stitch will also go from back to front, with the thread forming a series of diagonal lines across the edge of the fabric.

MACHINE SEWING

If you've never used a sewing machine before, please allow us to introduce you. Although Shannon will be the first to admit she's not exactly fond of machine sewing, she will also admit that a machine can make things go a heck of a lot faster.

Sewing machine stitches differ from hand stitches in that instead of one thread going over and under the fabric, machine stitches are made of a top (needle) thread interlocking with a bottom (bobbin) thread. This makes the sewn line much more stable. Machine sewers control the length of their stitches by adjusting the stitch length on their machine. The stitch-length control knobs on most machines are numbered 0 to 5. The smaller the number, the smaller the stitch. The average stitch-length setting is 2.5. When in doubt, leave it set there.

One great thing about thrift stores is that you can often find a sewing machine two aisles down from the clothes you want to alter! Garage sales are a great place to find one, too. Always plug it in before you buy, though. We're big fans of old-school metal machines, which are often cheaper and better made than the newer plastic ones. (In fact, Shannon's mom was made an offer she couldn't refuse for her old metal Singer when she took it in for repairs. She traded in the more-than-thirty-year-old machine for a good bit of change toward her new one!)

When you flip the power switch and press the foot pedal, the needle, or where the needle should be if it's missing, should move up and down with ease. Look out for frayed power or foot-pedal cords. If the needle is missing, that's not a big deal. They're cheap and easily replaced.

MAKE FRIENDS WITH
YOUR SEWING MACHINE

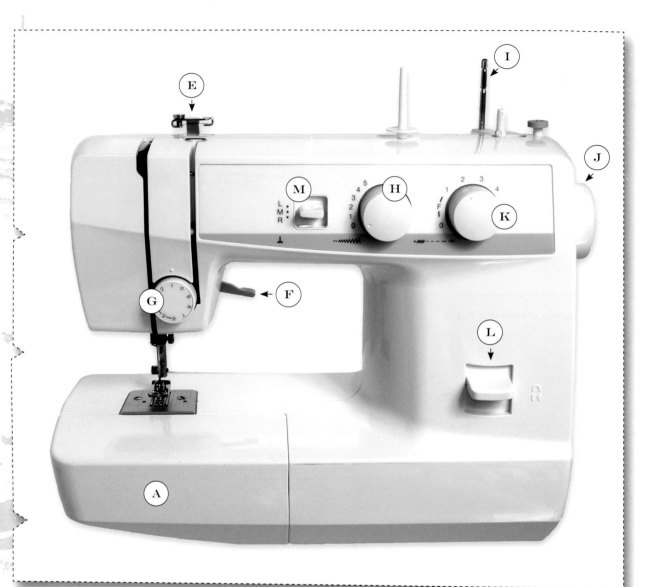

A. *bobbin case*

B. *feed dogs* (see opposite page)

C. *presser foot* (see opposite page)

D. *needle* (see opposite page)

E. *thread guide*

F. *thread uptake lever*

G. *tension control*

H. *stitch patterns*

I. *thread spool pin*

J. *hand wheel*

K. *stitch width selector*

L. *power switch*

M. *stitch length selector*

Sewing Machine Needles

There are several types of sewing machine needles made for sewing on everything from heavy Lycra to T-shirt jersey, denim and delicate silk. The main differences are the shape of the point, from rounded to very sharp, and the size and shape of the eye. When in doubt, refer to your owner's manual or ask an employee at your local fabric store which needle will work best for your project.

The Bobbins

Bobbins are the Robin to your sewing machine's Batman. Small and forgettable, yet utterly necessary, the bobbin functions as a tiny reusable thread spool that feeds thread to interlock with the needle thread as you stitch along. When you switch to a new thread color in the needle, you'll also need to switch to a matching thread in the bobbin (unless you like the two-color look: try it out on a scrap piece of fabric with two very different colors of thread in the needle and bobbin). When you go to buy spare bobbins, take it from us: Bring along one you know fits your machine. Sewing machines are finicky and each type will take one—and only one—kind of bobbin. It's no fun to get home and discover the twenty bobbins you just bought won't fit.

When you're winding a new bobbin, be sure to use the bobbin winder thread guide or its equivalent on your machine. (Check the manual. If you've bought the machine at a garage sale or inherited it from a great-aunt, you can search online; many sewing machine manuals are available as free PDFs. Start with the manufacturer's Web site and go from there. Or, if you like having a print copy, search eBay.) You want the bobbin to wind its thread on as evenly as possible so it will feed evenly for each stitch while sewing; otherwise, you're just asking for trouble.

The Tension Control

Your sewing machine works best when the tension is set correctly. Sloppy tension makes stitches look too loose, tight, or anything but "Goldilocks" (just right). The tension control on the top or front of your machine will help you adjust the top tension if things look other than perfect.

To test the tension, grab a spare piece of fabric or (if you're sewing something thrifted and don't have extra fabric) test in an out-of-the-way location. First, stitch with the tension set as is. Look at the stitches on both sides of the fabric. If you see loops of bobbin thread on the top side of the fabric, turn the top tension control down a notch. If you see loops of needle thread on the bobbin side, turn the top tension control up a notch. Every fabric is different, so it doesn't hurt to test the tension for each new project.

If adjusting the top tension doesn't do the trick, check your machine's manual or look online for additional instruction.

The Thread Guide

Maybe your tension is off because you missed a thread guide somewhere. The thread guide keeps tension on the thread as it feeds down into the needle, and keeps your stitches even and happy. Check your manual or the Internet for threading instructions.

The Stitch Pattern and Width Selectors

The stitch pattern selector on some machines gives you a number of pretty stitches to play with: everything from embroidery stitches to automatic buttonholes. Even if you don't have a lot of fancy stitch patterns to choose from, almost every machine out there has both a straight stitch and a zigzag stitch. The zigzag is used on knit fabrics such as T-shirt jersey because it has a lot of give that moves and stretches with the fabric.

The stitch width selector lets you set the width of your zigzag stitches. As a rule, you'll want to use a narrow zigzag for sewing seams on knit fabrics and a wide zigzag to finish a raw edge. If you don't have a serger (see page 18), this is the stitch you'll use where serged edges are called for. Experiment with a spare piece of fabric and the stitch width selector to see what your machine can do with a zigzag stitch.

Some machines have the zigzag and straight stitches as the same stitch pattern, but setting the width to zero makes a straight stitch, and numbers above zero give you a zigzag.

PREVENTING A RAT'S NEST OF THREAD

When you start a line of stitching, sometimes the thread will suddenly tangle up into a messy nest of thread where the stitches should be. To keep this from happening, pull the bobbin and needle threads out 1" (3cm) or so behind the needle and hold on to them for the first few stitches.

The Stitch Length Selector

The stitch length selector allows you to adjust the length of your stitches. For sewing on most fabrics, use a stitch length between 2 and 3 (about 10–15 stitches per inch). On T-shirt jersey, use a slightly higher stitch length. Too short a stitch on knit fabrics can sometimes cause puckery seams. If you set the top tension a little loose and set the stitch length as long as your machine will allow, you can get a nice basting stitch that's easy to pull out.

The Presser Foot and Feed Dogs

The presser foot and feed dogs are the bread in your fabric sandwich. The presser foot keeps the fabric down flat against the feed dogs, and you have to have it in the down position any time you are pressing the foot pedal to stitch, or you'll end up with a real mess. (Try it on a spare piece of fabric if you don't believe us.) The feed dogs help the fabric move as you sew. The tiny gripper teeth rotate to pull the fabric along under the presser foot as stitches are made.

The Reverse Button

Make note of where the reverse button is on your machine. When sewing a seam, it's a good idea to reverse at the end and sew back over the seam for four or five stitches. Think of this (called backtacking) as a little drop of glue to keep the stitches from unraveling.

The Foot Pedal

And finally, the foot pedal. Easy does it. Don't be tempted to put the pedal to the metal until you know just how responsive your foot pedal is. Some are super-sensitive to the touch, others less so. Better to be tentative when you're just getting to know your machine.

FLYING NEEDLES AND THE ZIGZAG STITCH

Before setting the stitch width above zero for zigzag stitch, be sure to take the straight-stitch foot off your machine and put on the zigzag foot. Also, if there's a straight-stitch throat plate on your machine, be sure to swap it out for the zigzag throat plate.

You will know instantly if you forget to do this, because your needle will hit the foot or the throat plate with a nasty thud, and break. Not only is this annoying, it can be dangerous if the broken needle flies up and hits you in the eye.

SERGERS

A serger is a specialized type of sewing machine that trims off the edge of your fabric while simultaneously sewing a seam and wrapping multiple threads over the edge of the fabric. Are you wearing a T-shirt right now? Flip up the bottom or your sleeve and look at the edges. Almost all clothing made from knit or jersey-style fabrics is sewn with a serger because it prevents the fabric edges from raveling. You can use a serger on almost any kind of fabric, and it's a big time-saver. We used a serger on many projects in this book, including the T-shirt Dress on page 70 and Mamma Mia! Shrug and Skirt Set on page 32. In most cases, a zigzag stitch can be used in place of a serger stitch. If you enjoy sewing, investing in a serger is well worth the money.

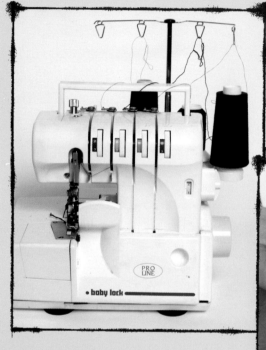

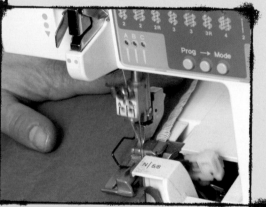

HOW TO AVOID TRASHING PINS, NEEDLES AND SERGER BLADES

Sewing over pins on your sewing machine is like running red lights. You may get away with it for a while, but sooner or later you're going to hit something. If you hit a pin, it will be bent beyond use. No big loss. When the needle hits a pin, either the needle will break or its point will be trashed. Either way you'll have to replace it. Be sure to pull the pins out one at a time, before you sew over them.

Sewing over a pin with a serger is a guaranteed disaster. The pin will be sliced in two by the serger blade. You'll have one trashed pin, one trashed serger blade and possibly one injured eye. For serging, always place the pins at least ½" (13mm) away from the raw edge of the fabric and parallel to it.

CUTTING

Cutting fabric is easy as long as your equipment is sharp. A good pair of sewing scissors goes a long way. Leave the scissors meant for paper on your desk; they'll dull quickly, and cut badly! Expect to pay twenty (U.S.) dollars and up for decent scissors. If you're left-handed, definitely shell out for a lefty pair.

Rotary cutters look like they're meant to cut pizza, but they're excellent for working with everything from thick fabrics like felt and wool to the most delicate cottons. To use them, place the fabric on a self-healing mat and press down with the rotary cutter wherever you want to cut. You'll see self-healing mats hanging next to the rotary cutters at the fabric or craft store: buy the largest one you can afford, because it's annoying to constantly readjust the fabric or the mat when cutting large pieces. They also come in handy for quick measurements, as most mats feature a printed grid on top. If you want to cut perfectly straight lines, use an acrylic ruler (sold next to the rotary cutters and self-healing mats).

IRONING

A good iron is truly your best friend! Make sure it has multiple heat settings and the ability to turn steam on and off. We don't recommend cordless models—they lose heat too quickly and may take twice as long to do what you need to do. If you don't have an ironing board, you can always put a layer of towels on a table, but it will be more difficult to iron some fabrics perfectly flat; besides, you risk scorching your table.

When you read instructions for a sewing project, keep in mind that there's a difference between "ironing" and "pressing." Ironing is just what you think it is: sliding a hot iron back and forth over fabric, usually pressing down on the iron at the same time. Pressing involves pressing the iron down on one spot, then lifting it before moving to another spot. Stretchy fabrics should be pressed to keep from distorting the shape. You always want to press, not iron, fusible web and fusible interfacing (see page 20) to keep the melting goo and fabric pieces from sliding out of position.

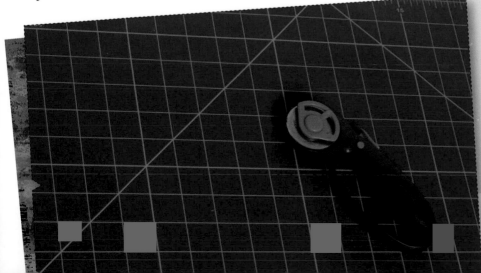

ROTARY CUTTERS AND TRIPS TO THE ER

This is no joke. Rotary cutters are a sewer's best friend and the most dangerous tool in your sewing kit. Even an old dull blade is razor sharp. Never, never—let me repeat that: never—put your fingers in the line of fire of your rotary cutter. Never cut toward your fingers or your hand. When using an acrylic ruler to guide the rotary cutter on tough fabric like denim, be aware that using the necessary pressure can cause the cutter to slip and take a good slice out of the hand holding the ruler.

One more thing: Make a habit of closing the protective cover around the blade every time you put the rotary cutter down, even if it's just for a minute. Nothing is worse than accidentally grabbing the business end of an unprotected blade or having a curious kitty bat at it.

FUSIBLES: SEWING WITH YOUR IRON

Fusible web is a kind of heat-activated fabric glue. It's a whisper-thin webbing that comes in rolls ½" (13mm) wide and in sheets by the yard (or meter). It's used to fuse fabrics together. You can do an emergency hemline fix by pressing a strip of fusible web under the hem. It beats staples any time. Strips of fusible web (sold under the names Stitch Witchery and Steam-A-Seam) are handy for holding fabrics together while you stitch them. In some cases, fusible web may be used to hold fabrics together permanently, but if any stress will be placed on the fabrics, it's better to also sew them. Sure, you could make the *T-shirt Dress* (page 70) with just an iron to connect the pieces, but we wouldn't advise it. Fusible web holds up well, but not *that* well. (Do you really want to risk having your skirt fall off in public?)

Fusible web is not to be confused with fusible interfacing, which is a knit, woven, or nonwoven fabric with heat-activated glue on the back. It's used inside collars, cuffs, waistbands and any other garment parts that need added body or structure. Fusible interfacing comes in a puzzling array of types and weights. If you want to give it a try, look for someone at the fabric store who looks like they know what they're doing and ask if they can help you pick the right one.

Both fusible web and fusible interfacing are finicky about they way they want to be handled. Using either too much or not enough heat, and leaving the heat on either too long or not long enough can cause the glue to fail. Your best bet for good results is to carefully follow the instructions that come with your fusibles.

EXPERIMENTING WITH T-SHIRTS

T-shirts are cheap, readily available and fun to play with. Use them as basic ingredients to experiment with techniques you might want to use elsewhere.

The Art of Manipulating Fabric by Colette Wolff is an amazing reference book that will give you ideas for every possible way to gather, shirr, ruffle, tuck, pleat, ruche, quilt or otherwise manipulate fabric into different shapes. You can apply quite a few of these techniques to the humble T-shirt, either short- or long-sleeved. Here are some ideas to play with.

Ruching

Basic ruching (pronounced *rooshing*) is done by gathering one or more vertical lines of stitching, such as on a side seam or down the top of a sleeve. Polyester thread is best for this because it doesn't break easily.

STEP 1 | Mark one or more vertical lines where you want the ruching. You can space them regularly or irregularly; both ways look great. Cut some thread about 4" (10cm) longer than the first line, and knot the end.

STEP 2 | Insert the needle in one end of the first marked line, and take one tiny backstitch to anchor the thread. Sew along the line with stitches ⅛–¼" (3–6mm) long. Leave the thread tail loose at the end of your line of basting. Repeat step 2 for each marked line.

STEP 3 | Going back to the first marked line, pull on the thread tail to gather the fabric, spreading it evenly as it begins to pucker up. When you're done gathering, don't tie off the thread yet. Repeat this on each of the lines you marked. When all of your lines are gathered, fiddle with the gathers until you like the way they look, then tie off the threads and trim the tails.

Fabric Paint

Ever made a tie-dye shirt? Most people use rubber bands to mark off the various puckers and gathers of fabric before dipping the shirt into dye, and that's that. You can do something similar with fabric paint. Try pleating a piece of fabric by folding it back and forth like a fan, then stitch the tops of the folds together and paint metallic fabric paint on the top ridges. Allow the paint to fully dry. When the stitching is removed, only the metallic pattern will remain on the fabric's surface.

Now, let's tie these techniques together. You can make a simple bolero-style shrug out of a long-sleeved T-shirt just by cutting off the bottom and opening up the front, as in the *Mamma Mia! Shrug and Skirt Set* on page 32.

Ruche the long sleeves of the T-shirt to three-quarters of their original length. Fan-fold the body of the shirt and apply fabric paint as described above. See how easy it is to combine techniques? You can take elements from several different projects in this book and combine them into all-new concepts.

For a cropped top that doesn't show all, cut off a T-shirt's bottom and add a wide piece of lace trim or fabric. Or, for that belly dancer look, add fringe!

You can also crochet a lacy edging or sew on embellishments such as beads, ribbon or other trim. And be sure to check out the excellent range of iron-on stitch guides made by Sublime Stitching. They're designed for embroidery, but you can also paint or apply beadwork along the lines.

You can cut off the neckband of a T-shirt asymmetrically (some cheaply made T-shirts have miserably tight neckbands, making this a great solution), or just scoop it farther down. Let the fabric roll back on itself if it's thin, or turn about ½" (13mm) of fabric under and stitch around the opening with small stitches. Use embroidery floss for a dash of extra color.

Experiment! When you're cutting up cheap thrift-store tees, you can afford to play.

A GIRL AND HER GROMMETER

We use a lot of grommets in this book; they're those metal rings that you see on corsets and other laced-up garments. Got a pair of Converse shoes handy? Those are metal grommets around the laces. Xan's been a fan of grommets for years and now she's gotten Shannon hooked, too. For one thing, corset lacing can make just about any garment sexier. Don't believe us? See the *Office Corset* on page 44. And if you happen to gain a pound or two, you can just loosen your grommeted shirt or skirt a smidge instead of consigning it to your closet (or back to the thrift store!). Grommets are highly decorative, come in many different colors (though gold and silver are most common) and are very durable once set. If you don't already have a grommet setter, a word of advice: Buy the hammer-set type, not the squeeze type. Hammer grommet setters are exactly as they sound. You place the male and female grommets on either side of the hole in your fabric and whack them together with a hammer or mallet. Hammer grommet setters often come complete with a hole-making tool as well, which comes in handy when you're making a garment with many grommets (no, paper punches won't work on fabric!). Squeeze grommet setters rely on your hand and grip strength, which can be less reliable than a mallet. Trust us, once you get hooked on grommets, you'll love them, too.

STEP 1 | GATHER MATERIALS

Gather your materials. In addition to the grommets themselves, (for the hammer set method) you will need a hammer, the setting tool and either a thick piece of leather or a stack of newspapers to pound on.

STEP 2 | PUNCH HOLES

If your grommet setter does not have the ability to punch holes in fabric (this one does—you simply put the fabric on top of your leather or newspaper stack and hit the punch with your hammer), you will need to cut appropriately-sized holes for your grommets. Put the male side of each grommet through each hole in the fabric.

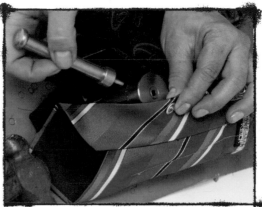

STEP 3 | INSERT FEMALE SIDE

Use your hands to press the female grommet side onto the back of each male grommet.

STEP 4 | PREPARE TO SET GROMMET

Hold the grommet sides in place with your fingers to prepare for the setting, and line them up onto the base of the grommet setter.

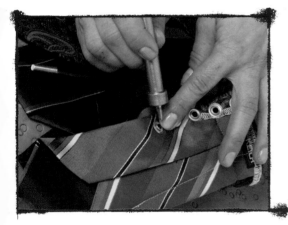

STEP 5 | INSERT SETTER

Carefully insert the upper portion of the grommet setter.

STEP 6 | SET GROMMET

Hit the setter gently but firmly with the hammer.

GARAGE SALE BLOOMINGDALE'S

Ah, garage sales and thrift stores. Shannon used to be embarrassed when her mother showed such outright glee about them, until she grew up and realized spending $80 for a designer shirt you're going to wear twice before spilling tomato sauce on it is just stupid—not to mention boring. You can find more original, fun stuff to wear in your average Goodwill or Salvation Army store than in a year at the mall. It's all in knowing how to put things together, and alter them to your taste. Most of us can't get away with wearing a 1960s silver lamé cocktail dress in public, but they sure are fun to cut up and use as trim. Coupled with the basics (good jeans, white T-shirts, black cardigans, fun shoes), you can't lose. Buy something wild and make it your own.

Not all finds are good ones. That hopelessly stained leather jacket is going to cost more to dry clean than to buy, plus there's no guarantee the stains will come out. (You can always paint over them, though—see page 62). But if you want to cut up the back to make a bag, or use the unstained sleeves for something else, OK. Know the piece's limitations.

Ditto shoes. If they don't fit now, they won't later. We can't tell you how many pairs of too-tiny John Fluevogs, Doc Martens and Steve Maddens Shannon's mom's has found for her in brand new condition over the years. The day plastic surgery foot reductions become possible will be a very happy one in her house!

Anything fabric is fair game, including shrunken sweaters. Skirts can become larger or smaller, shirts can lose or gain sleeves, Necklines, buttons, lengths—all completely changeable. Beware of stains, however, particularly perspiration stains. Once set, they're not coming out, no matter what some crazed Australian tells you on TV. In fact, they may change color for the worse if you try to bleach them out.

A common problem for anyone over size 10 is that many thrift store finds are too small. In the less fancy garage sale environment, all the larger sizes tend to sell out first, too. Some of the projects in this book will give you ideas for using grommets or clever additions of fabric strips to enlarge that dream skirt or those fabulous pants, but as a rule, shirts are usually more trouble than they're worth, particularly if they're fitted.

Keep an eye out for materials you might not have thought to use: The housewares section, for example, will often yield gently-worn sheets with great patterns, perfect for making everything from tops (see the *Bedhead Top*, page 36) to a skirt (see the *Asymmetrical Sheet Skirt*, page 104). Where else are you going to find David Hasselhoff/*Knight Rider* pillowcases these days?

A NOTE ON PROJECTS

The projects in *AlterNation* are divided into sections based on the article of clothing being created, with techniques for extra methods and tips that didn't quite fit in anywhere else sprinkled all over. We don't repeat how-tos in every pattern: how to add grommets, for example, is shown once, even though several patterns feature grommets. And if you can hem the edge of a cut shirt sleeve, you can hem the bottom of a skirt; it's the same concept on a larger scale.

Remember: This book is meant to give you *ideas*, not a set of rules. If you can't find the exact items we used, adapt accordingly. Thrift stores vary widely in quality and contents. You can find tons of wool sweaters for cheap in the Midwest and Northeast, but not in Los Angeles; experienced thrifters know which Goodwill stores are worth combing and which aren't. If you're trying to duplicate the things we've made exactly, you're missing the point. Make these ideas your own, then share and show them off! Visit www.alternationbook.com for more inspiration.

SHIRTS

The six shirt patterns in this section transform T-shirts and buttondowns, introduce a number of decorative techniques, tools and sewing methods, and give you ideas that can be applied to many other projects. T-shirts are a particularly great starting point for experimentation: They're cheap, widely available in a massive range of sizes, colors and prices, and everyone loves them. Admit it: somewhere deep inside your closet you've got a tour shirt for your former favorite (now embarrassing) band, or a camp T-shirt from the summer before eighth grade. Why allow them to simply take up closet space when you can make those well-worn cotton friends into something new and cool?

The lowly T-shirt has gotten a lot of love in the past year or two; we've lost track of how many T-shirt transformation books have been published, not to mention online tutorials by the dozen. Why is that? Consider the anatomy of a shirt. At the most basic level, you can alter the sleeves, sides, neckline or bottom of a shirt by chopping them off or lengthening them. You can also combine multiple shirts into one new work of fashion art, add images, beading, fringe or other trim. Melissa Dettloff of www.lekkner.com makes amazing clothes out of nothing but reconstructed T-shirts; check out her Web site if you need inspiration, or read the "Experimenting with T-shirts" section (page 20) for even more ideas. Paired with simple pants or jeans, a stylish shirt will always look good. Shirts are the perennial backbone of your fashion wardrobe, so kickstart your brain and let's go!

JACKIE O'S YACHT SHIRT

This is a super-simple technique that can be used with any T-shirt and any scarf or scrap of fabric. By using contrasting fabric (whether contrasting in color, material, texture or all of the above), you add visual interest to what was formerly a basic, blah shirt.

MATERIALS

T-SHIRT
SQUARE 10" × 10" OR 12" × 12" SCARF OR BANDANA
MATCHING THREAD
MEASURING TAPE
SCISSORS
SEWING NEEDLE
STRAIGHT PINS
SERGER (OPTIONAL)

1 REMOVE SLEEVES

Turn the shirt inside out and cut the sleeves off, leaving about ¼" (6mm) of the sleeve fabric past the seam. Preserving the seams when removing the sleeve will help keep the material from raveling when the shirt is washed. Turn the T-shirt right side out.

2 ALTER SCARF

Measure the armhole opening, and the diagonal measurement across the scarf. Cut across the scarf diagonally, and trim it so the long side of the triangle is equal or slightly longer than the measurement of the sleeve opening. Serge or zigzag stitch the raw edge to keep the threads from raveling later.

3 FOLD EDGE UNDER

Fold under about ½" (13mm) along the serged edge of the scarf and pin the fold. With the T-shirt right side out, line up the center of the scarf piece on the T-shirt's shoulder seam.

4 PIN SCARF TO ARM OPENING

Keep the folded edge of the scarf just covering the sleeve seam on the right side and pin the scarf to the front and back of the sleeve opening. For extra "flutter," don't attach the scarf around the entire armhole opening. Repeat for the second sleeve.

5 SEW SCARF TO SHIRT

Sew the scarf pieces onto the sleeve opening. Serge or zigzag stitch the remaining raw edges of the scarf and the sleeve opening. Or fold the raw edges of the scarf under two times and sew them with a simple straight stitch. Finish the remaining raw edge of the sleeve opening in the same way.

VARIATION: URBAN LEOPARD SHIRT

For this variation, the step-by-step techniques are the same, but the sleeves are shaped and attached in a slightly different way. Instead of triangular sleeve shapes, you've got rectangular ones. Check out the difference:

The scarf piece used for the Urban Leopard shirt was cut into a square rather than a triangle. This view of the flutter sleeve from below shows how it's attached to the armhole opening. Rather than create a full sleeve, you attach it to the upper two-thirds or so.

Another view of the sleeve from the side, showing how long this particular sleeve is. (Of course, you can also make them much shorter—using just a wisp of fabric—if you'd like.)

MAMMA MIA!
SHRUG AND SKIRT SET

You don't have to be pregnant to love maternity gear. This rosy shrug and skirt set was made from a lightweight pullover V-neck maternity sweater. Maternity sweaters are sized normally on top, but have plenty of extra fabric around the bottom that can be transformed into skirts, wraps or any other tube-shaped creation, such as the T-shirt Dress (page 70).

(page 70)

MATERIALS

MATERNITY SWEATER

APPROXIMATELY 1 YARD (1M) OF 1" (3CM) WIDE ELASTIC FOR WAISTBAND

FUSIBLE WEB, ½" (13MM) WIDE (OPTIONAL)

MASKING TAPE (OPTIONAL)

THREAD

MEASURING TAPE

SAFETY PIN

SCISSORS

STRAIGHT PINS

IRON (OPTIONAL)

SERGER (OPTIONAL)

SEWING MACHINE OR NEEDLE

VINTAGE PIN, FABRIC FLOWER WITH PIN BACK OR ELASTIC LOOP AND BUTTON FOR CLOSURE (OPTIONAL)

1 CUT SWEATER

Cut the sweater into two pieces according to the illustration above. Be sure to measure for the length of the skirt before you cut! Notice that the shrug in the photo had to be cut very short so there would be enough left for the skirt. In this case, our sweater had a V-neck to start with, but if yours doesn't, you can always shape the opening accordingly.

2 FINISH RAW EDGES

Now you can either serge the raw edges of each piece to seal the edges as we've done here, or fold the edges under and stitch them closed using a either a straight stitch or a hand-sewn whipstitch (see page 13). In either case, pinning helps to keep the edges even.

If the sweater fabric is flimsy and difficult to sew, try using thin fusible web to hem the edges. Cut a piece of fusible web the length of the shrug's bottom opening (extending to the top of the neckline if you've cut the fabric and left a raw edge instead of using an existing V-neck such as this one). Pin the fusible web to the wrong side along the raw edge of the opening. Be sure to insert the pins point in from the edge of the shrug, so you can pull them out as you fuse the hem closed. Fold the edge over to the wrong side, then press to fuse the hem in place, pulling the pins out as you go. Then stitch along the raw edge. You need to stitch the edge down after fusing it; otherwise, it may come loose with wear or washing.

MEASURE ELASTIC

3

After ensuring that the top edge opening of the skirt has been cut straight across, measure around your waist with a piece of elastic. When measuring elastic for a waistband, it should be slightly stretched until firm against your waist but not overly tight. If your waist is 30" (76cm), for example, the elastic piece may be 29" (74cm) cut but 30" (76cm) stretched. It's better to cut it a little too long than too short—you can always trim it later. Different widths of elastic are used for different purposes. In this case, with a thin knit sweater fabric, we used a piece 1" (3cm) wide. (A thicker sweater fabric would require a slightly wider, more "powerful" piece of elastic to stand up to its bulk.) Cut the elastic to the appropriate length.

FOLD TOP OVER

4

Turn the skirt inside out and fold the top of the skirt over 1½" (4cm). Pin the folded-over edge into place. This will give you a readymade tube to thread the elastic into.

SEW WAISTBAND TUBE

5

Sew a seam around the top of the skirt ¼" (6mm) in from the raw edge. So you have a way to get the elastic inside the tube, leave about 1½" (4cm) open at the end of this seam. If sewing this seam is problematic for you, try using masking tape to keep the fabric in place and give you a guideline for stitching. Depending on the fabric, you might prefer to use your machine's zigzag stitch option; the stretchier the knit fabric (especially if there's Lycra in it), the more useful a zigzag stitch is in preserving the fabric's elasticity. Check the stitch selector knob on your sewing machine and turn it to the zigzag before you begin to sew. If you're stitching by hand, don't worry about it: Handsewn stitches are not usually as rigid as machine stitches, so they won't affect the fabric's elasticity as much. Sew your seam along the top.

In the photo here, the top edge of the skirt has been folded over, pinned into place, and sewn down using a straight stitch. We serged the bottom edge with a decorative lettuce stitch, but if you don't have a serger, you can fold it over to the inside of the skirt and stitch it down as you did the top.

6

INSERT ELASTIC

Pin a safety pin to the end of the elastic and use it like a sewing needle to thread the elastic through the tube. In the photo for step 5, you see the opening that was left after sewing the seam along the top of the skirt. This is where you will thread the elastic through the tube, and come back around through the other side. When the elastic is through, use the safety pin to connect both sides of the elastic and try on the skirt. Trim the elastic if necessary to get a good fit, then overlap its ends and stitch them together. If you are machine stitching, go back and forth over the joint several times.

7

CLOSE TUBE

To finish the skirt, all you have to do is close the open ends of the tube where you threaded the elastic. This is generally too small and fiddly to do by machine. It's easiest to sew this by hand with a whipstitch.

To close the shrug, you can use a vintage pin, make a fabric flower with a pin back, or sew on an elastic loop and button. Our model chose to wear it open, which also looks great.

SEAM ALLOWANCES

Seam allowances are the extra bit of fabric past a line of stitching. (Commercial patterns usually tell you how much of an allowance is built in to that particular pattern.) The standard seam allowance in garments is ⅝" (16mm) for woven fabrics and ¼" (6mm) for knits. As a general rule, it's a good idea to leave at least ½–1" (13–25mm) fabric any time you sew two pieces of fabric together. It's easier to trim off excess fabric than rip out a seam and resew it! (And if you sew too close to the edge of the pieces, that's probably what will happen.)

BEDHEAD TOP

This halter top was made out of a pillowcase, taking advantage of its basic shape. The plainer tank variation merely carves out armholes and a neck opening, but for extra va-va-voom, open up the back and finish it with corset-style lacing. Although the basic shape is very simple, it has a lot of potential. For more flounce, you can pick apart the side seams and insert godets (see below), or add sleeves similar to those on Jackie O's Yacht Shirt *(page 28). The model is wearing an* Asymmetrical Sheet Skirt *(page 104).*

MATERIALS

PILLOWCASES

2 YARDS (2M) COORDINATING ½" (13MM) WIDE RIBBON TO LACE UP THE BACK (FOR FITTED VARIATION)

10 GROMMETS

TAILOR'S CHALK

THREAD

GROMMET SETTER

MEASURING TAPE

SCISSORS

SERGER (OPTIONAL)

SEWING MACHINE OR NEEDLE

Note: *You may need a friend to help you cut the armholes.*

WAITING FOR GODET

What's a godet? Godets are triangular panels inserted into the bottom of a piece. They add width without distorting the measurement at the top of the cut where they're inserted. If made in a lighter-weight fabric than the piece they've been added to, godets will sometimes be hidden while the wearer is standing still, but magically appear with movement.

1 TRACE PATTERN

Trace the armholes and neckline of an exsisting tank top onto a pillowcase. Don't mark the armholes too deep.

2 CUT TO SHAPE

Cut the armholes through both layers of fabric, but only cut the front of the neckline through one layer of the pillowcase. Cut a slit in the front neckline just long enough to get your head through it. Ask a friend to trim the armhole to the shape you want.

3 MARK ADDITIONAL CUTTING LINES

On the back of the pillowcase, mark a line across the back at the armholes. Draw another line down the center.

4 CUT PILLOWCASE OPEN

Cut along the two marked lines and open the back of the pillowcase.

5 CUT STRAP

To make the halter strap, mark a line about 3" (8cm) from the top of the pillowcase and cut along that line to trim away the rest of the back.

6 TRIM TO SHAPE

Fold the halter strap up and trim the corners to give it the shape you want. To make the top a little more fitted at the waist, mark lines like the dashed lines in the drawing. Trim the neckline to a shape you like, then serge or zigzag stitch all of the raw edges.

7 ADD GROMMETS

Mark where your grommets will be placed on both sides of the back of the halter top. It is important that your grommets line up. Place the top on a flat surface with the two edges of the back together. Starting at the top, use a straightedge to measure down 1" (3cm) and in from the edge 1" (3cm), and mark that space. Do the same on the opposite panel. Measure down 2" (5cm) and mark again. Continue down every 2" (5cm) until you have marked 5 grommet placements on each back edge. These should line up. Set the grommets according to the instructions on pages 22–23. Lace ribbon from the top down, and tie in a bow at the bottom to wear.

VARIATION: SIMPLE TANK TOP

This closed-back tank is flattering on slim, boyish body types or on children. If
have a large bust or prefer a looser style, opt for the grommeted, lace-up version.

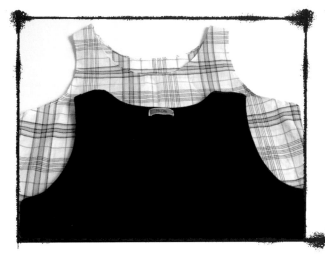

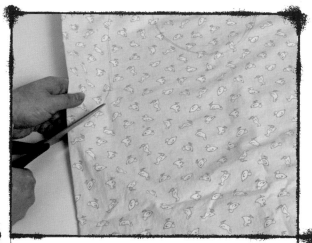

STEP 1 | CUT ARMHOLES AND NECKLINE

*Cut openings just large enough for your head and arms.
You can either cut small holes, try on the pillowcase
and have a partner trim away excess fabric around the
arm and neck until it's the shape you want, or trace an
existing tank top, which is what we did here.*

STEP 2 | FINISH RAW EDGES

*Either fold the raw edges of the arm opening under to
stitch closed, or serge the open edges if you have a serger.
That's all! If you have small children, these make really
great romper-style dresses, although you may need to make
the waist a little smaller with elastic or a ribbon tie.*

CUSTOM PHOTO BUTTONDOWN

Combining multiple craft techniques in one shirt, this men's buttondown features a photo printed on cotton with an ordinary ink-jet printer and fringe trim available by the roll at fabric stores.

WHITE BUTTON-DOWN SHIRT OR T-SHIRT

WHITE 100 PERCENT COTTON FABRIC

DIGITAL PHOTO OR OTHER COMPUTER-GENERATED IMAGE

DECORATIVE TRIM AND/OR EMBROIDERY THREAD

BUBBLE JET SET AND BUBBLE JET RINSE (SEE THE GUIDE, PAGE 140)

FREEZER PAPER

FUSIBLE WEB

THREAD

SCISSORS

FRONT-LOADING INK-JET PRINTER

IRON

SEWING MACHINE OR NEEDLE

Note: *If you prefer, you can buy printer-ready sheets of pre-treated fabric at most craft or fabric stores.*

1 PREPARE FABRIC
To prepare your own fabric for printing, first treat it with Bubble Jet Set according to the manufacturer's instructions. When the fabric is dry, iron the wrinkles out, then use the iron to press freezer paper onto the fabric, placing the waxy side on the wrong side of the fabric. Remove the freezer paper, and trim the fabric to a standard size that fits in the printer.

2 PRINT IMAGE
Feed the paper-backed fabric into a front-loading printer, one sheet at a time. Ink-jet ink is water soluble and needs to be "set" in the fabric. Allow the printed image to dry, then soak the fabric in Bubble Jet Rinse according to the manufacturer's instructions. Allow the fabric to dry, then press it.

3 ATTACH IMAGE
Attach the printed piece to your shirt using fusible web (sandwiched between the image and the shirt). This will provide a nice stiff surface for embroidery and other stitching if you want to add them.

4 ADD TRIM
Now you're ready to add trim and embroidery, if you like. Sometimes the simplest stitches are best. Try outlining something in your picture with a simple running stitch, or making colorful little asterisks to fill in a background.

THE ART OF WASHING ... ART

Sometimes the artwork created with decorative techniques like these is not quite as stable as a commercially-printed shirt. Test the colorfastness of your art before stitching it down, or attach snaps to the back of the art and the front of the T-shirt, so you can remove the art before washing the shirt.

FELT + T-SHIRT = FABULOUS

Craft felt is fabulous stuff. If you don't believe us, check out www.saltlicknyc.com—their T-shirts are amazing. But sometimes we don't have the patience to cut out lots of tiny shapes, and we want the felt to do the work for us. Enter fancy embossed craft felt! We found this over near the upholstery materials at our local fabric store. It was heat-embossed at the factory. If you've ever pressed down too hard with an iron and left dent marks on fabric, you've got the idea.

Don't limit yourself to just shirts! You can attach shapes to hoodies, sweatshirts (see the Day of the Dead Jacket, *page 56), even skirts. But craft felt is not the most durable substance around, especially if the shapes you've cut out are delicate, so handwashing is recommended. Or, for extremely large or delicate shapes, make the art removable by attaching snaps to the back.*

MATERIALS

T-SHIRT

CRAFT FELT

EMBROIDERY THREAD OR BEADS (OPTIONAL)

FUSIBLE WEB (OPTIONAL)

THREAD

SCISSORS

STRAIGHT PINS

IRON (OPTIONAL)

SEWING MACHINE OR NEEDLE

1 CUT SHAPES

Cut out shapes you like. (With this felt, we followed the basic shapes of the embossed pattern.)

2 PIN SHAPES IN PLACE

Pin the shapes into place on the T-shirt. If the craft felt is very thin, you may want to attach it to the shirt using fusible web and a hot iron first. Or, for multi-layered, 3-D shapes made of different felt colors such as flowers, you may want to fuse them together into their final layout before attaching them to the shirt.

3 SEW FELT TO SHIRT

Stitch the shapes down with a straight stitch around the outer edges, using embroidery thread for extra color if you're hand sewing. You can even add beads or other embellishments: Felt daisies and other flower shapes look especially nice with a beaded center.

Scholastic *plus*

43

OFFICE CORSET

Transform an ordinary buttondown shirt into a saucy corset-style top with just a few grommets and some ribbon. We were thinking about Jennifer Perkins's shop name (Naughty Secretary Club) when we were first sketching ideas for this book, and we wondered just what exactly a naughty secretary might wear. (Check out www.naughty secretaryclub.com, by the way, for superstylish accessories and much more.) You can use either a men's or women's buttondown, but the latter will require much less shaping.

MATERIALS

BUTTONDOWN SHIRT

4 YARDS (4M) ½" (13MM) WIDE RIBBON

FUSIBLE INTERFACING

GROMMETS

THREAD

WASHABLE MARKER, TAILOR'S CHALK OR QUILTING PENCIL

GROMMET SETTER

HAMMER (OPTIONAL)

LEATHER PUNCH (OPTIONAL)

MEASURING TAPE OR RULER

SCISSORS

IRON

SERGER (OPTIONAL)

SEWING MACHINE OR NEEDLE

1 REMOVE SLEEVES
Remove the sleeves. Turn the shirt inside out and cut the sleeves off just past the seam that attaches them to the body, leaving an extra ½"–1" (13mm–25mm) of fabric.

2 FINISH RAW EDGES
Fold the cut edge where you just removed the sleeves under once (twice if the fabric is extra-delicate or thin), iron it flat and pin it into place. Stitch around the edge with a straight stitch. If you have a serger, you can serge the edge, then turn it under and stitch it down inside the armhole opening.

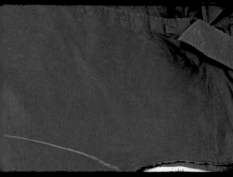

3 OPEN SIDE SEAMS

Open the side seams (underneath the armpit) by cutting or using a seam ripper. Better-made shirts have the raw edges in the side seams enclosed in felled seams, so cutting may be your only option. Start at the bottom of the shirt and work your way up to the armpit.

4 SHAPE THE SIDES (OPTIONAL)

If you're starting with a men's buttondown, you may want to shape the sides for a more feminine look. Using another shirt or dress that fits you closely, place it on top of the shirt and trace the curved shape from under the arm to the bottom of the shirt. If you don't have an appropriately shaped shirt to use as a template, measure the halfway point between the underarm seam and the bottom of the shirt, and mark 1½" (4cm) in. Draw a curve from the underarm to the bottom of the shirt, with the widest point at that 1½" (4cm) mark.

Pin or baste along the curved line, then try on the shirt. Does it fit better? Are there any gaps? If you're high-waisted, you may need to adjust where the widest part of the curve sits. Unpin (or tear out the stitches) and re-pin as needed until the shirt is as form-fitting as you desire. Now you're ready to cut. Leaving an extra ¾"–1" (19mm–25mm) (depending on how much excess fabric remains outside the curve), cut outside the line you've established and continue with the rest of the steps.

5 ADD INTERFACING

Fold the raw edge under ½" (13mm) on each side of the openings under the arms and press a crease along the fold. (You can also serge it and fold the serged edge to the inside.) Cut a thin strip of fusible interfacing and position it on the wrong side of the fabric along the pressed crease, as shown. Then, fold the raw edge over the interfacing. This interfacing will build up the fabric's thickness and stabilize the edge to provide a foundation for the grommets. It will help the fabric hold up better in the long run.

6

WHIPSTITCH SIDES

Whipstitch the open sides of the shirt together loosely and try the shirt on again. If you're happy with the fit, continue (the sides can either just touch each other or you can have an inch of free space between the two if you're comfortable with showing skin!). Leave the sides stitched together for now. This will make it easier to line up your grommets in pairs.

7

MARK SPACING FOR GROMMETS

Mark where the grommets will go using tailor's chalk or a washable quilting pencil on the interfacing, matching pairs on either side of the opening, with a grommet's width of space between each one vertically. Putting a measuring tape or ruler that has identical markings on either edge is a simple way to make sure your spacing is even. You can use just a few grommets, or opt for a lot of them, as we've done here.

8

INSERT GROMMETS

Using your marks as a guide, punch holes in the fabric. Many grommet setters come with a tool to make the hole. If yours didn't, use a leather punch and a hammer. Set the grommets according to your grommet tool's directions. (See "A Girl and Her Grommeter," page 22, for further instruction.)

 If you don't want to use grommets, you could make buttonholes instead (many sewing machines have a setting that will make them for you automatically).

9

ADD LACING

Starting at the top, thread the ribbon into the grommet holes, shoelace-style. Tie a large bow at the bottom if you'd like.

JACKETS

One stunning jacket can make an outfit, whether you're wearing a slinky black dress or a tank top and jeans. Lightweight or leather, denim, corduroy, khaki—jackets are a fashion staple you shouldn't underestimate!

These fashion pieces are both functional and decorative. While they're keeping you warm, they also keep you stylish. Keep an eye out for jackets in unusual colors or materials. That 1970s faux alligator jacket might look stupid on the rack, but superfly when the spread collar is covered with contrasting fabric. You never know until you try.

The jackets you'll see here are only the beginning. Use the techniques, such as reverse appliqué (*Reverse-Appliqué Suit Jacket*, page 64), to liven up any other piece in your closet, too. Cotton crochet cutouts (see *Spiderweb*, page 61) would look particularly cool on a pair of jeans, and fabric paint (see *Painted Suit Jacket*, page 62) isn't just for fluffy 1980s sweat-shirts anymore.

KATHMANDU JACKET

Tired of the same old denim? Cut off your jacket sleeves and replace them with hand-knit or crocheted sleeves made of sari silk, then add a sari-inspired fabric panel to its back. We used recycled sari silk yarn from Mango Moon (www.mangomoonyarns.com), a company that provides jobs for many Nepali women. They spin yarn made of junked (shredded) used saris, so each skein is completely unique, varying based on the fabrics that went into it. If you can knit or crochet in the round, you can make this project easily—and if you can't, the learn-to-knit suggestions in The Guide (page 140) will point you in the right direction.

MATERIALS

DENIM JACKET

3 SKEINS MANGO MOON RECYCLED SARI SILK YARN OR 600 YARDS (550M) OF SIMILAR BULKY YARN

½ YARD (46CM) SARI-STYLE INDIAN-PRINT SILK FABRIC

THREAD

CIRCULAR KNITTING NEEDLES, U.S. SIZE 10 AND 13 (6MM AND 9MM) ON 12" OR 16" CORDS (30CM OR 40 CM)

MEASURING TAPE

SCISSORS

STRAIGHT PINS

SEWING MACHINE OR NEEDLE

1

PREPARE JACKET

Cut off the existing sleeves on the jacket, leaving an extra 1"–2" (3cm–5cm) past the shoulder seam to preserve the seam. Wash the jacket, which will cause this cut edge to fray and fluff up. Leave the frayed fluff, but trim off any long strings.

2

KNIT SLEEVES

• Knit a 4" (10cm) gauge swatch with the yarn you chose for your sleeves and size 13 (9mm) needles. Count how many stitches make up 4" (10cm) and divide by 4 to determine the number of stitches per inch (or by 10 for stitches per centimeter). (Note: If you do use sari silk yarn to make your own sleeves, you should know that it's considerably heavier than wool or other fibers. Once off the needles, it will stretch a little under its own weight. When using the very general guidelines given here for knitting your own sleeves, you may want to stop just above your wrist rather than right at it. Unlike wool, this yarn won't spring back automatically when washed!)

• Measure around your jacket's armhole opening.

• Cast on the appropriate number of stitches to fit your armhole opening on size 13 (9mm) circular needles [either 12" or 16" (30cm or 40cm) cord on the needles will work]. For this sweater, we cast on 50 stitches. Join to knit in the round, being careful not to twist the stitches.

• Knit several rows, then hold the cast-on end up to the arm opening. Is it too big? Too small? You may need to adjust the number of cast-on stitches to match your own personal knitting gauge. If your knit piece is a little bit bigger than the opening, you can "squoosh" the stitches together at the top when you stitch the sleeve on. If it's too small, though, you'll be stretching the arm to fit, so you may want to start over and cast on a few more stitches.

• Knit until the tube reaches your elbow.

• Switch to size 10 (6mm) needles, knit until the tube reaches your wrist, and bind off.

• Repeat for the second sleeve. Set the sleeves aside.

3 ARRANGE PRINT FABRIC

Place the Indian-print fabric on the back of your jacket so you're happy with how it looks. Depending on the print, you may want to arrange it so the print runs sideways, or the selvedge runs vertically—don't feel restricted by the direction in which the print is supposed to go! This particular fabric had a very cool brocade pattern that just lent itself to going straight across the top.

4 CUT FABRIC TO SHAPE

Cut the fabric out around the "frame" formed by the back seams of the jacket, leaving 1" (3cm) of extra fabric all around past the frame to be tucked under and sewn. If the fabric is slippery like this one, you'll want to fold the extra fabric allowance underneath and press with an iron (put a towel on top to keep from scorching the delicate fabric if you're using silk or a synthetic blend fabric).

5 PIN AND SEW FABRIC

Pin the fabric into place. Sew the fabric down inside the "frame."

6 PIN SLEEVES TO JACKET

Pin the sleeves to the armhole opening as follows:
• Mark the front and back halves of the sleeve with two pins in the armhole end of the sleeve.
• Turn the sleeve right side out and the jacket inside out. Slide the sleeve inside the jacket and match one pin to the shoulder seam on the jacket. Put the edge so it overlaps the jacket's seam by 1" (3cm) and pin the sleeve at the shoulder seam. (The overlap will give the top of the sleeve a little support and keep the knit fabric from pulling or gaping when your arm moves.)
• Think of a clock, with the shoulder seam as noon.
• Pin at the underarm seam (6:00).
• Next, mark the sleeve at 3:00 and 9:00 and pin these to 3:00 and 9:00 on the jacket.
• Continue to pin clockwise at 1:30, 4:30, 7:30 and 10:30, making sure you have equal amounts of knit fabric between each pin.

7 SEW SLEEVES

Attaching the knit sleeves to the jacket is actually easier to do by hand than by machine. Thread a needle with your matching thread (we used black, which blended into the multicolor sari silk yarn) and push it through where the shoulder seam of the jacket meets the extra fabric you left when cutting off the sleeves. Pull it up through the knit fabric, being sure to get behind both pieces of yarn on the cast-on edge, and stitch back down into the sleeve as if to whipstitch. Work your way around, then repeat the process for the second sleeve.

DON'T KNIT?

Don't knit? (That's OK, Shannon promises not to be offended—she'll even teach you how if you ask nicely!) Cut the sleeves off an existing sweater—natural-colored cable knits are particularly nice—and stitch them on instead. If the sweater was sewn together with a machine or serger, be sure to cut the sleeve off so the serged edge is preserved. This will help keep it from raveling later on. If you like, you can then attach part of the sweater body to the back of the jacket, or felt it and cut out flowers or other shapes to sew on as decorations! Or combine multiple sweater colors and textures for even more color.

WHAT IS A SELVEDGE?

Good question. The selvedge is the long edge of a woven fabric. The word derives from the term "self edge," the edge naturally created by a loom's weaving action. Cotton fabrics meant for quilting often have the fabric and manufacturer's names printed on the selvedge.

TENTACLE JACKET

Shannon loves felting, particularly when it comes to recycling old sweaters into new, cool garments. This jacket was inspired by her work on a felted pillow for another book, Amy Swenson's Not Your Mama's Felting. *The Octopillow featured raised felted tentaclelike shapes, and so does this jacket. Consider* Tentacle *the "daughter of Octopillow." If you are looking for extra inspiration with this shaped felt technique, check out Nicky Epstein's* Knitting Never Felt Better *or Shannon's* Felt Frenzy *(with Heather Brack) for additional ideas. The possibilities are truly endless.*

MATERIALS

DUSTER-LENGTH (MIDCALF) SWEATER-JACKET, AT LEAST 50 PERCENT WOOL

HEAVY COTTON CROCHET YARN OR COTTON KITCHEN TWINE

THREAD

VARIOUS PLASTIC LIDS (WE USED SODA AND ORANGE JUICE BOTTLE LIDS)

SCISSORS

SEWING NEEDLE

STRAIGHT PINS

SERGER OR SEWING MACHINE

WASHING MACHINE AND DRYER

1 CUT OFF SLEEVES

Cut the sleeves off your sweaterjacket. If it has a hood, as this one does, cut it off, too. You don't want either one to shrink when you make the "tentacles" on the jacket body itself. When cutting the sleeves off, leave the shoulder seam on the cut-off sleeve itself to keep it from unraveling. Set them aside.

2 WRAP FABRIC AROUND LIDS

Plan where you would like your "tentacles" to be. Wrap the jacket body around the plastic lids one by one. Stretch the knit fabric as tightly as you can, and tie each lid off with cotton yarn or kitchen twine (it must be cotton or else you risk felting it into the jacket itself).

3 WASH JACKET

When you're pleased with your tentacle arrangement, wash the jacket only (no sleeves or hood!) once or twice using a hot wash and cold rinse until the fabric is so shrunken you can no longer make out individual stitches. Air dry or put in the dryer.

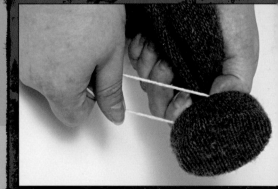

4 REMOVE LIDS

Cut off the cotton ties and pull out all the lids. You can stop here and leave the distorted fabric as "bubbles," or press the center of each bubble down inside itself and stitch around the outside of the circle to form tentacle shapes. Experiment with different styles.

5 REATTACH SLEEVES

Pin the sleeves (and hood, if you have one) back onto the jacket body and sew them on. (See page 53, step 7.) If the arm openings got distorted during the washing and drying process, you may need to iron them out a bit (sometimes felt can press itself into wrinkles in the washer). We used a serger, but you could also use a sewing machine and stitch the pieces on with a ½" (13mm) seam allowance.

DAY OF THE DEAD JACKET

This jacket is both comfy and stylish. You can reshape an ordinary crewneck sweatshirt, as we've done here, or apply the decorative techniques to a hoodie that already fits you nicely. We used motifs cut from a larger piece of Mexican-inspired fabric; you could also use patches or iron-on designs.

MATERIALS

CREWNECK SWEATSHIRT, SLIGHTLY BIGGER THAN YOUR SIZE

PRINT FABRIC

MASKING TAPE (OPTIONAL)

PAPER GROCERY BAG

WASHABLE MARKER OR TAILOR'S CHALK

MEASURING TAPE

SCISSORS

STRAIGHT PINS

IRON

SEWING MACHINE OR NEEDLE

***Note:** It will be easier to shape this jacket if you enlist a friend to help.*

1. MEASURE AND CUT SWEATSHIRT

Start by measuring from side to side of your sweatshirt and marking the center. If you're bold, you can cut straight up from the bottom; if you're not able to cut a straight line without help, mark the line with a washable marker or masking tape first. Cut off the ribbed cuffs and bottom, too. If you turn the shirt inside out, you can trim along the serged edge that attaches the ribbing to the main shirt body. Now you'll have a flat jacket shape.

2. REMOVE SLEEVES

Cut the sleeves off at the shoulder, just outside the serged edge. You're going to make the sides slightly smaller and fitted, which will alter the armhole a little bit. The sleeves will return later. Turn the shirt right side out.

3. SHAPE SIDES

Use the technique described in the *Office Corset* (page 46) to shape the sides. Take a shirt or dress that fits you closely, place it on top of the sweatshirt and trace the curved shape from under the arm to the bottom edge.

You can also measure the halfway point between the two and mark 1"–2" (3cm–5cm) in, depending on just how large the shirt is to begin with and how fitted you want the jacket to be. Draw a rough half-moon shape, with the widest point at that 1–2" (3cm–5cm) mark. Pin along this line (or run a line of basting stitches) and try on the jacket. (In the photo here, you'll see we began to pin on the right-hand side.) If you don't like the way it fits, unpin (or tear out the stitches) and re-pin until you do.

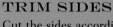

4

TRIM SIDES

Cut the sides according to your markings. Be sure each side matches the other!

CREATE DARTS

Next, make darts in the front and back (these are optional, but they make the jacket super-sexy—words you never thought would be applied to sweatshirt fabric). This may take a little experimentation; your jacket, and you, may be very different from ours size-wise, and everyone has personal preferences for fit. Find a sewing friend to help pin it while you're wearing the jacket and things will go much faster.

5

In this photo you can see that with the jacket inside out, we began to pinch and pin up two lines of fabric (which will eventually become shaped darts) on the jacket back. Once the side seams have been taken in, it's easy to determine how much fabric you should pin on these back darts. Once you are satisfied that your pinning is complete, finish by sewing.

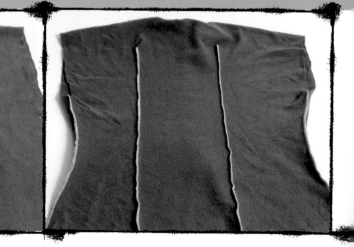

This is what your jacket should look like once the edges have been shaped, cut and sewn.

This is what your jacket should look like once the back darts have been sewn.

6

ADD PRINCESS SEAMS

Next, make a template of a very shallow curve (we like using paper grocery bags as templates, because they're strong and can be reused for future projects). If you're not comfortable with making your own curve template, ask your friendly local sewing store for a princess-seamed dress or shirt pattern and use it as a guideline. Mark a curve that extends from your armpit down the front to the hem. Use the same template to mark the back from the armpit to the hem. These lines will shape the jacket to fit you more closely than the sweatshirt did. This shaping is called a princess seam. The deeper portion of the curve pulls in the jacket at the waist, while the tapering at the top *allows room for your bust*. Pin excess fabric along the curve line to the inside of the jacket; each curve should mirror its twin on the other side. Now try it on. We won't lie. Shaping can be fiddly, which is why it's so much easier to do with a friend's help.

7

PIN AND SEW SEAMS

Using a technique similar to the one you employed on the back of the jacket, pinch the fabric along the curve established by your template shape (quilting and sewing stores often sell plastic templates that work well for this if you're not comfortable making your own) and pin, then sew as you did the back.

8

TRIM ARMHOLES

Trim off excess armhole fabric.

Almost done! This is how your jacket should look from the inside. When you get to this point, it's probably time for a celebratory mocha or something. Trust us.

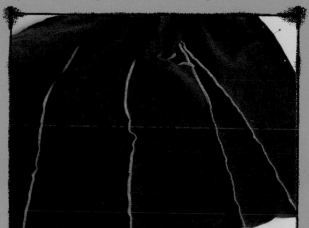

FIT SLEEVES TO ARMHOLES

When you're happy with the fit (or tired of being stabbed by so many pins—your call), sew the princess seams into place. Put the sleeves up against your new (smaller) armhole. The armhole will be smaller than the sleeve because of the princess seams you sewed. To make the armhole match the sleeve, trim off ¼" (6mm) all the way around the armhole. That doesn't sound like much, but you'll be surprised. If you need to enlarge the armhole a little more, trim another ⅛" (3mm) and continue trimming small amounts until the armhole is big enough. In the above-right photo, you can see how the armhole has been enlarged to fit the sleeve.

FINISH RAW EDGES

Fold under and pin the raw edges down the center front of the jacket. Pin the raw edges of the bottom and cuff openings under, then stitch around both. (Again, a sewing friend comes in handy here to make sure the bottom or cuffs aren't uneven.) Working from the wrong side of the fabric, stitch the raw edges down the center front of the garment and around the cuffs. Fold under, pin and sew the hem.

Now: the really fun part! Decide how you'd like to decorate your jacket. For the skulls, we cut out the shapes, pinned them down, then handstitched them (turning under the edges as we stitched. Give the jacket a light ironing and you're done!

9

10

VARIATION: SPIDERWEB JACKET

To create this variation you will make the jacket the same way, then embellish by adding cotton crocheted doilies or other odd bits of lace or interesting transparent fabrics (thrift stores are great places to find old lace!). Pin the doilies or scraps of fabric into place on the exterior of the jacket, then try it on to be sure you like the arrangement. Sew the pieces down, being careful to stitch all the way around each one. (If you're using crocheted or lace pieces without finished edges, turn the edges under and stitch them down as for the skulls in the *Day of the Dead Jacket.*) Finish by cutting away the jacket fabric underneath the lace from the inside of the jacket.

PAINTED SUIT JACKET

Shannon's always had a thing for oversized men's jackets, but they're not exactly the most feminine thing in the world. On a trip to Toronto, she spotted some altered suit jackets in the Kensington Market thrift shops that featured silkscreening, fabric appliqués and much more. (If you're a silkscreener or know someone who is, that's another technique you can use here.) So she asked her mom, Christine Okey, to paint one for her. Christine's an artist and thrift store score queen who dragged Shannon through a never-ending series of garage sales, thrift stores and consignment shops long before they were cool. She also happens to be quite handy with fabric paint. (If only her art school professors could see her now!)

MATERIALS

SUIT JACKET
(WE USED A MEN'S
JACKET FOR THAT
OVERSIZED LOOK)

FABRIC PAINT

GESSO
(OPTIONAL)

FLAT-BRISTLED
SMALL PAINTBRUSH

BEADS, LACE
OR OTHER
EMBELLISHMENTS
(OPTIONAL)

1 CLEAN JACKET

Prepping the jacket is key: Wash or dry-clean it first, then test your fabric paint on an inconspicuous location (under the lapel, on an inside seam, etc.).

2 PREPARE FABRIC FOR PAINTING

Assess your paint. Did it soak in really fast? When dry, is the color barely visible? If so, paint a layer of clear gesso over the area you plan to paint first. Gesso is used to prep artists' canvases; multiple thin layers are built up over time to give the canvas a smooth surface. It's available at art supply stores and also some craft shops. You could also try spraying the surface with a light coat of clear, matte spray finish, but don't use too much—you don't want the jacket to feel crunchy.

3 PAINT DESIGNS

Paint your designs. We did a simple freehand flower-and-vine motif, but you can paint whatever you want. Most fabric paint comes with a nozzle tip. If you aren't happy with the way the paint comes out, use your paintbrush to blend or spread it around. Allow the jacket to dry completely.

4 ADD EMBELLISHMENTS

Add beads, lace or any other embellishments you like. Bold vintage buttons are a nice touch. You can also hack the sleeves off to three-quarters length and hem them, or crop the bottom of the jacket for a more tailored look.

3-D EFFECTS

Resin craft is a really simple and cool way to add 3-D effects to your work. Resin comes in two parts that are mixed to create a chemical hardening reaction. One minute it's liquid, and the next it becomes a solid, clear plastic. You can make anything from buttons to jewelry to belt buckles with it. Look for it in craft stores.

REVERSE-APPLIQUÉ
SUIT JACKET

Reverse appliqué is a super-fun technique. You can do this on sweatshirts (as in the Spiderweb Jacket on page 61—just put the crocheted doilies to the back of the cutout instead), denim jackets, bags, sweaters—even pants! At its most basic level, you're cutting out a shape, putting another piece of fabric behind it on the wrong side of the fabric, and stitching the two together. If you choose a nonraveling fabric like the bouclé on this jacket, it's even easier, because you don't have to worry about the raw cut edge. Or, if you do it on denim, you can let the edge ravel and fluff up.

MATERIALS

SUIT JACKET (THE MORE BLAH THE COLOR, THE BETTER—IT MAKES THE COLLAGE POP)

ASSORTED FABRIC AND TRIM SCRAPS. (YOU CAN STICK TO A COLOR PALETTE, AS WE DID HERE, OR GO WILD.)

EXTRA FABRIC FOR LINING (OPTIONAL)

THREAD

SCISSORS OR ROTARY CUTTER

STRAIGHT PINS

SEWING MACHINE OR NEEDLE

CONSTRUCT FABRIC COLLAGE

Making fabric collage is fun, easy and a great way to use up fabric scraps. With a backing piece of fabric that sets the tone for the colors to come (in this case, hot pink), sew scraps of fabric on top of each other, stacking and layering until you like the way they look. The edges don't have to be perfect; in fact, the rougher they are, the more interesting.

If you have a sewing machine that does embroidery stitches, you can add those, too. Or if you have some really good thrift finds that are too beat up to use as originally intended (such as crazy quilts, a unique fabric or upholstery material), try putting them into a collage. Shannon's particularly fond of Rosemary Eichorn's book *The Art of Fabric Collage: An Easy Introduction to Creative Sewing* (see The Guide, page 140) if you need a jump-start for ideas. Your finished collage should be almost as big as the back of your jacket.

2 LOOSEN LINING

On this jacket, we loosened the inner lining across the bottom to make it easier to cut the heart shape out of the back. It will be stitched back in place after the appliqué is sewn down.

3 CUT OUT COLLAGE AREA

Cut the shape out of your jacket's back. We cut a large heart freehand. If you're not comfortable with cutting out shapes, try making a template out of grocery bag paper. Pin the template to the back of the jacket and cut around it.

4 PIN COLLAGE TO OPENING

Place the collage between the jacket lining and the wrong side of the jacket. Pin around the collage piece, following the edge of the opening in the jacket.

5 SEW COLLAGE TO JACKET

Stitch around the heart or other opening shape you cut, about ½" (13mm) from the raw edges.

6 RESTITCH LINING

Stitch the lining you loosened back down, if your jacket is lined. If you're using a denim jacket, you don't have to worry about a jacket liner, but if your collage is delicate, you might want to carefully stitch a solid piece of fabric to the inside of the denim to protect it from stress damage caused by movement inside the jacket.

DRESSES

Dresses are simple to make in all shapes and styles and they're a great solution to the daily what-do-I-wear conundrum. Just find a pair of matching shoes and you're out the door! They're also incredibly versatile as layering pieces, with jackets, sweaters or shirts on top, or with leggings or jeans or fancy tights underneath. We love dresses!

In this chapter, we'll show you a wide variety of dress-making possibilities using materials ranging from old T-shirts to men's shirts to even bedsheets. One of the beautiful things about a book like this is that you aren't limited in how you can apply the techniques you've learned up to this point. For example, any one of the dress patterns here could use, say, an image transfer like the *Custom Photo Buttondown* (see page 40), or perhaps a lace-up side panel like the *Office Corset* (see page 44). Try knitting long sleeves like those on the *Kathmandu Jacket* (see page 50) for a *T-shirt Dress* (see page 70), or adding silky scarf sleeves like those on *Jackie O's Yacht Shirt* (see page 28) to the sleeveless *Men's Shirt Dress* (see page 78). Feel free to experiment with mixing and matching your favorite new altering tricks with your favorite base project ideas.

T-SHIRT DRESS

Take three (or more!) T-shirts in colors mild or wild and shape them into this fun tube dress. It couldn't be simpler to make and it's lots of fun to wear. Don't limit yourself to solid colors, either—this could be your chance to make a Superfan Tour Shirtdress featuring all the live concert shirts littering the back of your closet. Or maybe a Cheesy 1980s Hair Metal Band Shirtdress. Mall Iron-On Shirtdress? Community Bowling League Shirtdress? Really, you could make about twenty of these and no two would be alike.

MATERIALS

3 OR MORE T-SHIRTS IN RELATIVELY SIMILAR SIZES (DON'T GO BY THE TAGS; MEASURE ACROSS FROM ARMPIT TO ARMPIT WITH EACH SHIRT STRETCHED FLAT.)

THREAD

MEASURING TAPE

ROTARY CUTTER OR SCISSORS

STRAIGHT PINS AND/OR MASKING TAPE

STRAIGHTEDGE (ACRYLIC OR METAL)

SEWING MACHINE OR SERGER

1 CUT THE FIRST SHIRT

First, decide which T-shirt will be the top of the dress. Unless you're going for a frayed or antiqued look, it should probably be the shirt with the nicest neckline (with no rips, stains or tears) or the color you like best closest to your face. With the shirt flat on a table, cut a straight line across it below the armpit. A rotary cutter and acrylic ruler will help you do this quickly and efficiently.

2 MEASURE WIDTH

Measure across the bottom of your top T-shirt and write down the width; you'll need this figure to adjust the other shirts.

3 CUT OTHER T-SHIRTS

Cut the remaining T-shirts the same way (you can save their tops for additional dresses, or cut them up to make fabric flower accents, appliquéd shapes—you name it). Keep the bottom tube portion intact.

4 MEASURE FABRIC TUBES

Measure across each tube portion and compare the width to the opening at the bottom of the first piece. Ideally, they should be the same as the first piece or slightly larger.

71

5 ADJUST TUBE WIDTHS AS NEEDED

If a tube doesn't measure as wide across as the piece you cut in step 1, this is not necessarily a bad thing. This is a good way to work more than three t-shirts into the design, especially if several of them are damaged or stained. Cut some sections from the tubes, and then piece the sections together into a wider strip. Sew this pieced strip into a new tube the same width as the top section of the dress. If a tube is larger by ½" (13mm) or more than the first shirt, turn the tubes inside out and sew a straight line down each one's side to adjust the size.

6 CUT DRESS COMPONENTS TO SIZE

Decide how wide you want the stripes on the body of your dress to be, and cut the tubes formed by the bottom half of the shirts accordingly.

7 ARRANGE CONSTRUCTION OF DRESS

This is the fun part: Rearrange the tubes until you have a stripe pattern that pleases you. If you want to try it on before stitching and without stabbing yourself with a million pins, tack the tubes together with masking tape before slipping it over your head.

8 PIN FABRIC TUBES TOGETHER

Pin the tubes together in the order you've selected.

9

SEW DRESS

Sew the tubes together. We used a serger to sew this dress, and so it can also be worn inside out (the contrasting stitching from the serger stands up like a row of embroidery between each tube). If you play your cards right and use the bottom of a T-shirt for the bottom of the dress, you won't even have to hem it!

10

SHAPE DRESS (OPTIONAL)

If the dress is a little big when you try it on, put it on inside out and pin the sides until the fit is to your liking (it helps to have a sewing buddy for this). Sew along the sides, turn the dress right side out and try it on again. If you have a similar dress that fits you well, you can also place it on top of this one and trace its basic shape to get the curves just the way you want them.

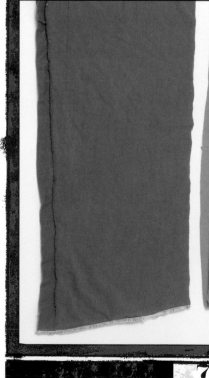

CRAZY-SIMPLE SHIFT DRESS

This dress is nothing but a tube with straps on top, when you think about it. If you're making it from a bedsheet, you'll fold the fabric in half lengthwise; if you're using cut fabric, you'll fold it in half with both cut sides as the bottom.

MATERIALS

FLAT BEDSHEET OR 3 YARDS (3M) OF 45" (114CM) WIDE FABRIC

THREAD

WASHABLE MARKER OR TAILOR'S CHALK (OPTIONAL)

SAFETY PINS

SCISSORS

STRAIGHT PINS

SEWING MACHINE, SERGER OR NEEDLE

Note: *It may be easier to shape this dress if you enlist a friend to help.*

1 MARK AND CUT OPENING FOR NECK

With your chosen fabric flat on the floor, place a T-shirt or tank top (recommended) at the top and pin it to the fabric with straight pins. Use the shirt's neck opening as a guideline to mark the neck hole for the dress. You can also use a round plate as a tracing template, or even an oval or square platter for extra interest. Remember, it's better to cut away less than you think you'll want—you can always cut away more when you try it on, but it's much tougher to add more fabric if you find that the opening is too big. Carefully cut the neck hole.

2 MARK AND CUT ARMHOLES

If you are using a tank top as a template, with it still pinned in place, use it to mark your armhole openings. (The same rules apply—cut away less than you think you need to.) If you are using a T-shirt with sleeves as a guide, mark a spot on your cloth aligned with where the T-shirt sleeve meets the shoulder seam at the top of the sleeve. Do the same at the bottom of the sleeve where it comes in to meet the side seam. Mark the curve for the arm holes between the 2 marks. A dinner plate works well; just line up the two marks along the edge of the dinner plate (curve facing into the garment), and draw a line along the edge.

3 PIN SHAPE

Using the shirt (still pinned to the sheet) as a rough guide for appropriate width, pin the lower section of the dress fabric together using safety pins along the sides of the shirt and down to the bottom edge. (Why safety pins? It makes the dress far less stabby when you try it on, which you'll be doing in the next step!) Pin together the shoulder area but not the armhole openings. Don't skimp; the more pins you use, the easier it will be to tell what parts need adjusting!

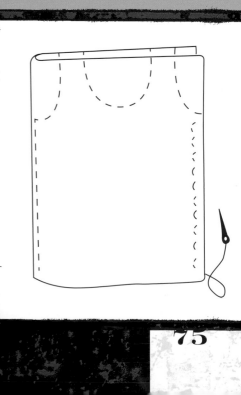

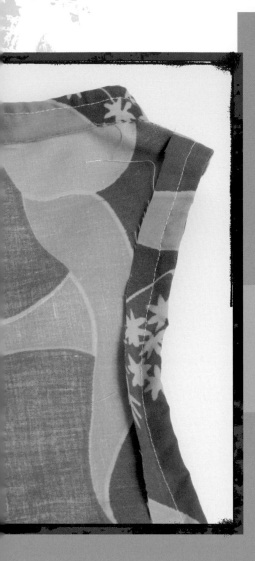

CHECK THE FIT

Slip the dress on and check the fit in a full-length mirror. Is it too big or small? Where? Re-pin as needed. With a little trial and error, you'll soon have an idea of where the fabric needs to be cut away, depending on your preferred fit.

If you have a sewing buddy, you can have her trace your outline on the fabric with washable marker or tailor's chalk. Pin 2"–3" (5cm–8cm) (or more, depending on how you like your fit) outside your outline and try it on. Or trace a dress you like that fits closely. Be sure to leave more fabric than you think you'll need from the waist down. Even though this dress is curvy, you'll be slipping it on over your head, so you need to be able to get it on over your shoulders and hips.

4

TRIM EXCESS FABRIC

Cut away the excess fabric and place the two pieces together with the right sides of the fabric together. Fold them over, lengthwise, and trim any excess to make sure both sides are equal. (If they aren't, the dress will be lopsided!)

5

PIN AND STITCH DRESS

Pin the sides together and stitch the top straps together. Sew the sides together from the bottom up to the armpit with a basting stitch. Turn the dress inside out and try it on again. You may need to trim away a little more fabric in some places. Baste the new seams, and try on the dress again. Repeat until the dress fits the way you want. When you're 100 percent happy with the fit, sew the sides closed with a straight stitch.

6

7

FINISH RAW EDGES

Tuck the armhole and neck openings under to the wrong side of the fabric, pin and sew. Fold the bottom under and sew the hem.

In this image, you can see how Xan used a tank top neck as a rough guideline for the neck and sleeve openings for the dress.

Using existing clothing as a cutting guideline is fast and effective. Instead of a T-shirt, Xan used a dress that fit her tightly to trace the shaping on the sides. If you don't like quite that much shaping, you can leave the sides straight.

VARIATION ON A THEME

Here's a variation that takes all the pinning guesswork out of the equation: Cut off the top of a T-shirt just below the bust (Empire style) and fold a sheet lengthwise. Cut the sheet to the length you want, measuring from below your bust to where the bottom of the hem should be, plus 2" (5cm). Run a line of stitches all the way across, 1" (3cm) from the top of the fabric. It's actually easier to do this by hand; use the strongest thread you have, such as a thick cotton thread (sometimes called rug thread or craft thread). Each running stitch should be about ½"–¾" (13mm–19mm) long. Sew the open long edge closed with a ½" (13mm) seam allowance. Now, pull the running stitch thread, gathering the top of the tube until it's the same size as the bottom of your cut T-shirt bottom. Insert the T-shirt, cut side up, into the top of the tube you just made from the sheet (which is inside out—the right sides of the T-shirt and the gathered tube should be touching). Pin the T-shirt bottom and the top of the tube together just below where you made the running stitch. Sew tube and the T-shirt top together. Remove the running stitch. Turn the dress right side out and voila! An Empire waist-styled sheet dress.

MEN'S SHIRT DRESS

MATERIALS

MEN'S BUTTONDOWN
DRESS SHIRT

SKIRT (OR YOU CAN
REMOVE AND USE
THE SKIRT PORTION
OF A DRESS)

THREAD

SCISSORS OR
ROTARY CUTTER

STRAIGHT PINS

SEWING MACHINE
OR NEEDLE

Have you ever had a favorite skirt whose top got damaged? (Thin Indian-print cotton skirts can be awfully rippy at times, as we've learned more than once ourselves.) It can be reborn with this dress pattern.

There are many possible ways to make this dress, and the look can vary widely depending on where you cut the shirt and skirt before joining them together. For a slightly high-waisted line, cut the shirt off at the bottom of your ribcage. For a very high-waisted Empire-look, cut just a few inches (or several centimeters) below the armpit. Sleeve length is another source of different looks. You can go sleeveless, as we did here, short or even three-quarter length; you'll hem them the same way in any case. And naturally, you can vary the length of the skirt, too. Make the skirt portion of the dress as long or short as you'd like—just remember to measure twice, cut once. Here we elected to create a skirt that falls just below the knee.

SELECT YOUR SKIRT

Pick a skirt that matches the style you want. It is best to avoid picking a tight, form-fitting skirt, especially if it has a zipper. There will be no way to include a zippered skirt unless you turn the skirt around to have the zipper in the front to align with the buttons. I suggest you use a skirt with an elastic band or one that buttons up the front (that will work with the buttons down the front of the shirt).

2 REMOVE SHIRT SLEEVES

Cut the sleeves off the shirt at your preferred length and turn the edges under. Stitch them down. Cut the excess bottom fabric off the shirt, and turn the shirt inside out.

PREPARE AND ATTACH SKIRT

Cut the old waistband off your skirt and turn the skirt inside out. Insert the shirt, cut side up, into the top of the skirt. The right sides of the shirt and skirt fabric should be together. Pin the shirt bottom and top of the skirt together, matching the raw edges.

If the skirt opening is considerably larger than the shirt bottom, you may need to adjust the skirt fabric equally around the bottom of the shirt. To do this, arrange the skirt fabric around the raw edge of the opening at the bottom of the shirt. Pin the two pieces together in one location (such as on a seam or at the center back). Think of the garment as a clock, with this first point as noon. Then pin at the opposite side (6:00). Next, continuing to line up the skirt fabric equally, pin the edges at 3:00 and 9:00. Continue to pin counterclockwise at 1:30, 4:30, 7:30 and 10:30, making sure you have equal amounts of fabric between each pin.

Stitch the tube closed, and turn the dress right-side out. That's all! You can sew a waist sash or belt out of excess skirt fabric if you like.

3

A NOTE ON PINNING

If you're hand sewing, it doesn't much matter how you place your pins, but if you're using a machine, you'll want to place them at a 90-degree angle to the raw edges being sewn together, with the pin heads facing out. This makes them much easier to remove as you're moving along, and it's less risky for your machine. Many a sewing machine needle has been broken on a stray pin!

SYNTHESIZE
T-SHIRT DRESS

This dress owes a lot to Jackie O's Yacht Shirt (page 28) and the dress techniques elsewhere in this section. If you like the style of this project, keep your eyes open for lightweight skirts that use interesting fabric colors or textures. They don't have to be exactly your style to work in this project. For example, combining a faded black heavy-metal or punk rock band T-shirt with a very "girly" pale pink print skirt offers an unexpected visual juxtaposition that's incongruous yet pleasing. You may be the miniskirt type, but don't overlook long skirts that can be shortened in a heartbeat.

MATERIALS

T-SHIRT

SKIRT, PREFERABLY
LONG AND FLOATY
TO GIVE YOU
ADEQUATE MATERIAL
TO WORK WITH

THREAD

MEASURING TAPE

SCISSORS

STRAIGHT PINS

SERGER (OPTIONAL)

SEWING MACHINE
OR NEEDLE

1 CUT T-SHIRT

Trim the hem off the T-shirt right above the stitches. Turn the shirt inside out and cut the sleeves off about ½" (13mm) past the seam connecting them to the main shirt body. Measure the armhole opening.

2 CUT SKIRT

Cut the bottom 5"–6" (13cm–15cm) inches off your skirt. Then, cut 2 semicircles of fabric out of the piece you cut off the skirt. The straight edge of the semicircle should measure at least as long as the shirt's armhole opening. These will become the new sleeves.

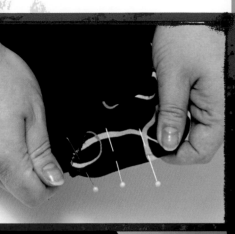

MAKE SLEEVES

Mark the center of the curve on a semicircular piece. Turn under the center of the semicircle about ½" (13mm). Pin the center of the semicircle to the right side of the shoulder seam of the armhole opening, as shown. Continue pinning the semicircle to the armhole opening, turning under the edge of the semicircle as you go. For extra "flutter," don't attach the fabric around the entire armhole opening, just at the very top portion of the shoulder and 1"–2" (3cm–5cm) down the front and back sides. Repeat for the second sleeve. Sew the semicircles of fabric to the armhole. Fold any remaining raw edges under two times and sew them closed with a simple straight stitch, whipstitch or serger (if you have one).

PIN SHIRT AND SKIRT TOGETHER

Pin the bottom of the T-shirt to the top of the skirt with right sides together. If the skirt opening is considerably larger, you may need to adjust the skirt fabric equally around the opening. Arrange the skirt fabric around the T-shirt opening. Pin the two pieces together in one location first, such as on a seam or at the center back. Think of the area to be pinned as a clock, with this first point as noon. Then pin at the opposite side (6:00). Next, continuing to arrange the skirt fabric equally, pin the edges at 3:00 and 9:00. Continue to pin clockwise at 1:30, 4:30, 7:30 and 10:30, making sure you have equal amounts of fabric between each pin.

5 CHECK FIT

Try on the dress to make sure you've pinned everything together evenly. It's OK to try it on inside out (otherwise you'll stab yourself with all those pins).

6 SEW DRESS TOGETHER

Happy with the way everything looks? Stitch the skirt to the T-shirt, and turn the dress right side out. Depending on the fabric, you may want to hem the bottom of the skirt, or you can leave it raw for that extra punk rock look.

BEYOND THE DRESS

Have leftover fabric? Cut it into long, thin strips and use it to lace up your favorite boots for a subtle, not too matchy touch.

85

SKIRTS

You name it, it can be made into a skirt. From corduroy pants legs to men's ties, even old jeans—when you've got some fun fabrics and have no idea quite what to do with them, skirts are the sewing project of choice. Whether a plain A-line or a flouncy, ballgownish affair, even the most die-hard pants fan will fall for these skirts. (And just to keep the pants fans happy, we've got some projects for you, too, in the next chapter.)

The Copper Cathedral Skirt (page 88) has fun with color and texture by using multiple pairs of corduroy pants to play colors and wale-widths against each other. (Note for fabric geeks: "Wale" is the term for the corrugated property of corduroy fabric itself. It refers to the width of the ribs, not the quality of the fabric. So fine-wale corduroy isn't necessarily better than wide-wale—its ribs are just thinner.)

Feeling a little Cinderellaish but don't want to dress up that much? (Glass slippers are pretty tough on your feet, after all!) Our *Denim Ballgown Skirt* (page 98) might be just the ticket. It's the perfect way to use up all those semi-destroyed pairs of jeans you can't bear to throw away.

But the *coup de grâce* in this section is Xan's *Tie Skirt* (page 92). *Coup de grâce* is a term that refers to the merciful, quick slaying of a wounded opponent during a swordfight. It's not misapplied here; you will absolutely bring the opposite sex to their knees when wearing these skirts—and garner a few envious looks from the girls, too. When we designed an entry for the Seamless computational couture show in Boston, Shannon wore one of these on stage with our model during the final curtain call, and it got even more attention than our model did! On the way out of the Museum of Science, someone yelled, "I love you, Tie Skirt Lady!" across the showroom. Believe us, you'll get attention when you wear these, too.

COPPER
CATHEDRAL SKIRT

The colors in this skirt remind us of the Tremont skyline. Tremont is a section of Cleveland (where we live) that has more Greek Orthodox churches than you can imagine. When you drive past the area on Interstate 71, you see a collage of patina-covered copper domes and brick—textured, weathered and glowing in the sun. We tried photographing this skirt with some of the domes in the background and it was hard to tell which stood out more!

MATERIALS

3 PAIRS OF CORDUROY PANTS IN COORDINATING COLORS

HOOK AND EYE

INVISIBLE ZIPPER (SEE THE TIP ON PAGE 91 TO DETERMINE THE LENGTH YOU'LL NEED.)

WASHABLE MARKER OR TAILOR'S CHALK

THREAD

INVISIBLE-ZIPPER FOOT

MEASURING TAPE

SAFETY PINS

SCISSORS

SEAM RIPPER

STRAIGHT PINS

STRAIGHTEDGE

IRON

SEWING MACHINE

Note: You may need a friend to help you fit the skirt.

1

CUT PANTS INTO PANELS

Cut the legs off of each pair of pants just below the crotch. Cut the side seam and inseam off each leg, cutting close to the seam to preserve as much fabric as you can. You'll have 6 panels which, depending on the original style and fit of the pants, may be roughly triangular (in the case of tapered pants) or rectangular (in the case of bootcut pants). Trim off the hems remaining from the original pants, then trim the panels so they're all the same length.

2

MEASURE AND MARK SKIRT PANELS

Math time! Measure your waist and add 6" (15cm) for seam allowances. Divide by 6. This is how wide each panel needs to be at the waist. Let's call this the panel width. Mark the center of the narrow end of each panel, then mark half the panel width to the right and left of the marked center. You're going to cut away the excess fabric past these marks.

Draw a line from each mark you just made to the bottom of the panel, and cut along these lines. You now have 6 panels to make into a skirt. Before you move on to the next step, mark the top of each panel so you don't end up sewing one in upside down.

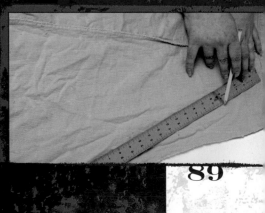

89

SEW PANELS AND CHECK FIT

Pin the six panels together, being sure to keep the top of each panel in the correct position. Stitch the pieces together with a ½" (13mm) seam allowance until all are connected into one flat piece. You will need your sewing buddy for this next part. Pin the last 2 panels together and try the skirt on inside out. Have your sewing buddy adjust the pins until the skirt fits the way you want it to, then use tailor's chalk to mark where the seam will go. If the chalk mark is ½" (13mm) from the raw edge, you're ready to go on to step 4. If the chalk mark is more than ½" (13mm) from the raw edge, trim the edges so they are ½" (13mm) from the chalk line. Don't sew the seam yet.

3

FINISH RAW EDGE

Use a zigzag stitch or serge the raw edge of the skirt waist. Fold under the edge ½" (13mm) to the wrong side, press lightly, and pin the fold in place. Sew around the skirt waist about ¼" (6mm) in from the folded edge.

4

BEGIN INSTALLING ZIPPER

Now you're going to sew an invisible zipper into your skirt. You will need a special invisible-zipper foot. They're inexpensive and can be purchased where you bought the zipper. Put the foot on your machine. With a very cool setting on your iron, open the zipper and press the zipper flat from the wrong side. Make sure the skirt is inside out. Pin the zipper tape (the cloth part of the zipper) face down on the right side of the fabric with the teeth on the seam line. Follow the manufacturer's instructions for positioning the zipper. Put the right groove of the invisible-zipper foot over the teeth of the zipper. As you sew, the teeth will stay inside that groove. Sew as far down the zipper as you can, then backtack to lock the stitches.

5

COMPLETE ZIPPER INSTALLATION

Pin the other zipper tape face down on the right side of the fabric with the teeth covering the seam line. Be careful not to let the bottom of the zipper get twisted. Put the left groove of the zipper foot over the teeth and sew as far down as you can.

6

90

7 SEW SEAM

Close the zipper and pin the seam down to the bottom. Make sure the end of the zipper is not caught in the pinned seam. Shift the needle position to the outer notch of the zipper foot. Sew the seam from just below the zipper to the bottom of the skirt.

8 HEM SKIRT

Hem the skirt as needed or leave it raw and let it fray— it's up to you!

INVISIBLE ZIPPERS

If you have sewn in a regular zipper, putting in an invisible zipper may seem a little inside out at first. But they are much, much easier to sew, and they look great. The package your invisible zipper comes in will have helpful instructions and good drawings to follow.

CHOOSING THE ZIPPER LENGTH

Zippers come in many different lengths. You'll probably want one in the 7"–16" (18cm–40cm) range, depending on the difference in size between your waist and hips. Wider hips require a longer zipper, so you'll have more wiggle room to get in. We know lots of women with tiny, tiny waists and big hips, so if you fit that description, buy a longer zipper.

TIE SKIRT

These skirts are Xan's signature piece, seen in galleries and boutiques from coast to coast. You can make them long, to wear like a traditional skirt, or abbreviated, to be worn over pants. West Coast boutiques seem to favor the shorter ones—probably because it's warm enough to wear them year-round! But these skirts tend to be showstoppers no matter where you live.

MATERIALS

MEN'S TIES (ANYWHERE FROM 16 TO 25...DEPENDS ON YOUR WAIST SIZE AND THEIR WIDTH)

GROMMETS

RIBBON (ENOUGH FOR LACING)

TAILOR'S CHALK

THREAD

GROMMET SETTER

HAMMER (OPTIONAL)

LEATHER PUNCH (OPTIONAL)

MEASURING TAPE

ROTARY CUTTER (OPTIONAL)

SAFETY PINS

SCISSORS

STRAIGHT PINS

STRAIGHTEDGE (OPTIONAL)

SEWING MACHINE

MEASURE AND ARRANGE TIES

Determine where you want the "hem" of the skirt to fall, measure from your waist to that point, and add 2" (5cm). Let's say that measurement is 14" (36cm) (yours might be different). Mark a line on each tie 14" (36cm) up from its tip. Make this the same on each tie, even if you plan to end up with an uneven hem later on.

Begin laying out the ties, slightly overlapping the edges. The ties will automatically form an arc (because of the way they taper from the tip to the cut ends). When you have some of the ties in place, if you want a staggered or a curving hem, you can begin staggering the tips, or slightly shifting each one as shown here.

Continue adding ties on each side until the top arc measures the same as your waist measurement plus about ½" (13mm). Pin the ties together where they overlap. Put the pins parallel to the edges of the ties so you'll be able to try on the skirt when the time comes.

93

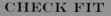

CHECK FIT

Wrap the pinned skirt around your waist, with the opening in the front. Check the hem length and see if you want it to be shorter or longer [remember that extra 2" (5cm) you left at the top of the skirt in step 1?]. Hold the skirt so it's the length you want. Mark one of the ties where your waistline is, then add 1" (3cm) above the waistline mark and draw a line around the top of the skirt. Trim any excess above that marked line.

Now it's time to check how the skirt fits. Does it overlap just a bit in the center front? You may need to adjust the ties slightly to get the overlap at the front and to get them to lie nicely. If you have to subtract a lot of length from the waist measurement, remove the center-back tie, or overlap some of the ties more than others. If you have to add to the waist measurement, add a tie in the center back and adjust the overlap of nearby ties.

SEW TIES TOGETHER

Now make sure you have all the ties adjusted the way you want them, and that the overlaps are firmly pinned for sewing. Use tailors chalk to mark a line across each tie 3"–4" (8cm–10cm) up from the tip. You will stitch your ties together down to this line. Remember, this is an asymmetrical skirt, so the line curves to take into account the lengths of the individual ties. If you are making a straight skirt with all your ties the same length, the line will be straight. Stitch down the length of each tie from the top to the white line, removing pins as you go. Then stitch across the top of the waistband, ½" (13mm) down from the top. You can serge or zigzag stitch the raw edge at the top of the skirt to hold everything firmly in place.

BEGIN CREATING WAISTBAND

Measure your waist (or just below, if you'd rather wear the skirt at hip level). Select 2 ties for the skirt's waistband. Open up the narrow end of each tie, pin the raw edges of the 2 ends right sides together, and sew them together. Wrap the ties around your waist with the tip ends in front. Mark the ties where they overlap about 4" (10cm) and trim the excess. This should give you a strip that will be longer than the final waistband.

CUT WAISTBAND

For the waistband, you now need to cut a strip about 3" (8cm) wide from the ties you sewed together in step 4. Steam press the waistband ties open flat. Mark and cut a 3" (8cm) band the length of the strip. (This is where a rotary cutter and straightedge come in very handy. If you use these tools, you don't have to mark where you are going to cut the band.)

2

3

4

5

6 FOLD EDGE UNDER

Fold under the raw edge about ½" (13mm) along the length of one side of the band and press a crease.

7 PIN WAISTBAND TO SKIRT

Match the raw edge of the waistband (without the pressed crease) to the top edge of the skirt with the right side of the waistband to the inside of the skirt. Remember, in step 4 you cut the waistband longer than your actual waist measurement? Center the waistband on the skirt, leaving some of that excess at each end. Pin the waistband to the skirt.

8 SEW WAISTBAND TO SKIRT

Place the waistband on the bottom against the feed dogs and the neckties on top under the presser foot. Sew the waistband to the ties, ½" (13mm) from the edge.

9 TRIM EXCESS FABRIC

At the end of the waistband, trim all but about ½" (13mm) of the excess fabric. Fold the remaining to the inside and pin it to hold it down. Repeat this on the other end of the waistband.

10 FINISH WAISTBAND

Fold the waistband toward the front of the skirt, tucking and pinning the raw edge under ½" (13mm) as you go. If you have already pressed under the edge, all you need to do here is pin the folded edge to the front of the skirt.

Sew the waistband to the front of the skirt about ¼" (6mm) from the folded edge. Add another line of stitching ¼" (6mm) from the top of the waistband.

11 ADD GROMMETS

Mark where the grommets will go, matching pairs on either side of the skirt front, with a grommet's width of space between each, vertically. You can use just a few, or many, whichever you think looks better. Punch holes in the fabric after you've marked each grommet's location. Many grommet setters come with a punch to make the hole; if yours doesn't, use a leather punch and a hammer. Set the grommets according to your grommet tool's directions; with our setup, you place the male and female sides of the grommet on either side of the hole and tap them together with a mallet. If you don't want to use grommets, you could make buttonholes instead. Many sewing machine models will do this automatically.

Starting at the top, thread the ribbon into the grommeted holes, shoelace-style, and tie a large bow at the bottom. Wear the grommets to the front, side or back—the skirt looks good from all sides!

95

DUAL-FABRIC SKIRT

Oh, the possibilities! We couldn't even possibly count the number of skirts you could make using this general idea. Pair denim with something slightly girly, khakis with cowboy-print cotton or corduroy with velvet. You name it—it'll look great!

MATERIALS

PAIR OF JEANS OR OTHER PANTS

EXISTING SKIRT

THREAD

SCISSORS

STRAIGHT PINS

SEWING MACHINE OR NEEDLE

1 CUT THE PANTS
Cut off the pants legs a few inches (several centimeters) below the crotch. Clip open the inseam and the crotch seam. Be sure to cut the stitches but not the fabric.

2 CUT NEXT TO FRONT CROTCH SEAM
Cut the fabric right next to the front crotch seam just past the curve.

3 CUT NEXT TO BACK CROTCH SEAM
Cut the fabric right next to the back crotch seam just far enough to open the curve.

4 OVERLAP AND SEW
Overlap the two sides of the front crotch seam and sew them together. Repeat this for the back crotch seam. You now have a miniskirt that's just a little too mini.

5 MEASURE AND CUT SKIRT
Use a drapey fabric for the lower skirt (we cut up a rayon wrap skirt). Measure the width around the bottom of the miniskirt. Cut the lower skirt at the point where the width matches the bottom width of the miniskirt.

6 SEW SKIRT PIECES TOGETHER
Turn the miniskirt inside out and keep the bottom skirt right side out. Slip the bottom skirt inside the miniskirt, matching their raw edges. Pin and sew them together.

97

DENIM BALLGOWN SKIRT

This skirt is so fun, not to mention much more flattering than the usual ultratight jeans skirts made from only one pair. Pair it with a simple tank, as seen here, or a plain white buttondown for a more preppy look. Big platforms or other dramatic shoes look really great with this skirt and let you keep it simple on top. After all, what's more classic than a pair of jeans and a white T-shirt? (Think of James Dean, Marlon Brando and other countless 1950s heartthrobs.) Shannon prefers the art of a finely made John Fluevog platform shoe, as her closet will attest (see www.fluevog.com for some examples).

MATERIALS

SEVERAL PAIRS OF JEANS (AT LEAST 4; 1 SHOULD FIT YOU WELL IN THE WAIST AREA)

THREAD

DENIM NEEDLE FOR YOUR SEWING MACHINE (OPTIONAL BUT HIGHLY RECOMMENDED)

SCISSORS

STRAIGHT PINS

SEWING MACHINE

1 CUT INSEAM OPEN

Start with the pair of jeans that fits you at the waist. Clip open the inseam. Be careful to cut only the stitches without nicking the fabric.

2 CUT CROTCH SEAM OPEN

Clip through the crotch seam and keep going down the other inseam.

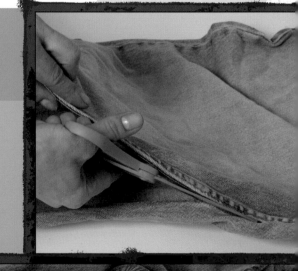

99

3
CUT FABRIC NEXT TO FRONT CROTCH SEAM
Cut the fabric right next to the front crotch seam just past the curve.

4
CUT FABRIC NEXT TO BACK CROTCH SEAM
Cut the fabric right next to the back crotch seam just past the curve.

5
OVERLAP AND SEW
Overlap the 2 sides of the front crotch seam and sew them together. Repeat this for the back crotch seam. You now have a skirt with absolutely no front or back. We don't recommend wearing it like this in public (although it would probably look pretty cool worn over a full skirt, like chaps).

6
MAKE INSERTS
Now you need to make inserts to fill in the front and back of the skirt. Cut the legs off a few old pairs of jeans; we used 3 for this skirt. Cut off the side seams of the legs (just whack them off—there's no need to slice through the stitches). This will be your first insert.

ADDING FLARE TO A SKIRT

The more pieces you fit into the open triangles formed by slicing open the side seams of jeans, the wider and more "ballgowny" your skirt will be. You can repeat the steps above by slicing up the side seams and inserting additional triangles of fabric as many times as you like!

POSITION FIRST INSERT

Lay the skirt out and spread the legs to create an upside-down V. Lay the insert under the V, fiddle with everything until it all lies flat, then pin the pieces together. Use plenty of pins at the point of the V so the fabrics don't slip when you sew them.

If there's a lot of excess fabric on the inside of the skirt around the insert, sticking out past the pins, turn the skirt inside out and trim as much of the excess as you can.

STITCH INSERT

Turn the skirt right-side out, and stitch from the hem to the point of the V. Every few inches (centimeters) as you sew, slide your hand inside the skirt and make sure the excess fabric of the insert is not getting caught up in the seam.

When you get to the point of the V, if you try to turn the skirt and sew down the other side, you'll be in for quite a wrestling match that you are bound to lose. Instead of doing combat with the skirt, backstitch about ½" (13mm) to lock the stitches. (This is more backstitching than usual, but there will be a lot of weight and stress on the seam.)

SEW OTHER SIDE

Remove the skirt from the machine, then sew the other side of the insert, stitching from the hem to the point in the V.

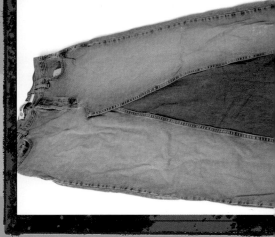

ADD ANOTHER INSERT

Repeat steps 6 through 9 to add an insert to the back of the skirt. For additional flare, you can add inserts (called godets) to the side seams of the skirt.

TRIM HEM (OPTIONAL)

If you want raveled fluff all around the bottom of the skirt, cut off any hems on the skirt and inserts. When you wash the skirt, the raveled fluff will become your hem.

DENIM CORSET SKIRT

This skirt—a technical hybrid of the Copper Cathedral, Denim Ballgown *and* Tie Skirt *on pages 88, 98 and 92, respectively— manages to become Best of Breed for all three! You'll use similar techniques to create the skirt, but end up with a whole new look.*

MATERIALS

1 3 PAIRS OF JEANS (DEPENDING ON YOUR WAIST SIZE.)

GROMMETS

TAILOR'S CHALK OR WASHABLE MARKER

THREAD

DENIM NEEDLE FOR YOUR SEWING MACHINE (OPTIONAL BUT RECOMMENDED)

GROMMET SETTER

HAMMER (IF YOUR SETTER REQUIRES IT)

MEASURING TAPE

SCISSORS

STRAIGHT PINS

SEWING MACHINE

RIBBON (ENOUGH FOR LACING)

1 CUT UP JEANS

Cut the legs off the pairs of jeans. Line up all the leg pieces with the hems oriented in the same direction and trim each piece to your desired skirt length plus 1" (25mm). Do not cut off the hems; these will become the waistband of the skirt.

2 DETERMINE YOUR MEASUREMENTS

Measure your waist and hips, and write the numbers down. If your waist and hip measurements differ by more than 2"–3" (5cm–8cm), trim your denim pieces into slightly triangular shapes so there is space to fit your hips without leaving excess fabric at the waistband. If not, you should be able to leave each piece more or less as is.

3 FOLD AND STITCH SIDES

Turn under 2" (5cm) of the raw edges on the sides of each denim piece and pin at the top and bottom. Sew the fold along the top of the piece and along the bottom. At the top, depending on how sturdy your machine and denim needle are, you may need to stop short of the stitching through the hem from the original jeans and stitch that down by hand later (some machines cannot handle that much thick fabric). Now measure the tops of the pieces. You need enough to go all the way around your waist. (So, if you have a 36" (91cm) waist and each piece is 6" (15cm) wide, you need 6 pieces.)

4 ADD GROMMETS

To finish, add grommets from the top edge of the skirt to a few inches (several centimeters) from the bottom on both sides of each denim piece. It's helpful to place the pieces next to each other and mark the grommet placement with chalk or washable marker so they'll line up when laced. Lace the sides together with ribbon, corset-style. Leave one side loose so you can pull the skirt on.

103

ASYMMETRICAL
SHEET SKIRT

This was made from the same sheet set as the Bedhead Top (page 36). If you want, you can sew a tank-style Bedhead Top to this skirt and make a dress, or just wear them as matching separates as shown here. I know we say all these designs aren't hard to make, but this one really takes the super-easy award. If you can fold a piece of typing paper and cut it to make a square, you can do this.

MATERIALS

TWIN-SIZED BEDSHEET

APPROXIMATELY 1 YARD (1M) OF 1" (3CM) ELASTIC FOR WAISTBAND

THREAD

WASHABLE MARKER OR TAILOR'S CHALK

MEASURING TAPE

SAFETY PINS

SCISSORS

STRAIGHT PINS

SERGER (OPTIONAL)

SEWING MACHINE AND NEEDLE

1

CUT SHEET INTO A SQUARE

Sheets are rectangular, but we need a square, so fold the sheet over evenly from the bottom corner to the side and cut across the top to obtain a square of fabric (see Figure A). (If you want, you can skip this step, but anything other than a square will probably be too long to walk in comfortably, not to mention really, really asymmetrical.)

2

CUT A HOLE FOR THE WAIST

Measure the waistband of a pair of pants that fits you well. Divide that measurement in half, and subtract 2" (5cm). This number is X. Fold the square of fabric over diagonally again to create a triangle. Think of the point formed in the middle of the folded fabric as the center of a circle, with X as its radius. Mark a 90-degree arc around the center point, then cut along the arc to make a hole for the waistband (see Figures B and C). Slip on the skirt. The opening should be at least 2"–3" larger than your waist, but it can be more; the larger the opening is, the more the elastic will gather it in. When you fold under the raw edge of the hole in the next step, it will enlarge the hole quite a bit.

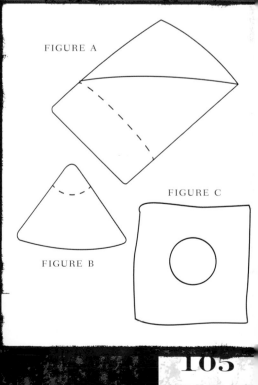

FIGURE A

FIGURE C

FIGURE B

105

CREATE A CHANNEL FOR THE ELASTIC

Fold the raw edge of the waist opening under to the wrong side about ½" (13mm) and score the crease with your thumbnail. Work your way around the circle this way. When you get back to the beginning, fold the edge under again about 2" (5cm) and pin. It's impossible to get this folded edge to lie perfectly flat. It will get a little twisty in places, but don't worry about it. Work your way around the circle and stop about 2" (5cm) from the starting point. Sew the folded edge down, leaving a 2" (5cm) opening where you will thread the elastic into the channel you've just made.

3

4

MEASURE ELASTIC

Wrap the elastic around your waist, slightly stretched. Overlap the ends a little and trim if necessary.

5

INSERT ELASTIC

Pin a safety pin at one end of the elastic and use it as a needle to thread the elastic through the channel. Make sure the elastic is not twisted. Bring the loose ends out on either side of the opening, overlap the ends and sew back and forth over them several times using the reverse lever on your machine. Stitch the opening in the channel closed to completely encase the elastic.

6

HEM SKIRT

Fold the bottom of the skirt over about ¼", pinning as you go. Hem the skirt by hand or machine.

PANTS

Pants tend to be much easier to alter than make from scratch. You can shorten them or lengthen them. (Got a closetful of Capri pants that are so last season? Add some fabric or lace trim.) You can add gems, iron-ons, embroidery or even appliqués—you name it. Or build a new pair from the ground up with a commercial pattern and that unusual fabric you found in the thrift store bargain bin—why not?

You can use a lot of the techniques shown in other types of altering projects to punch up your leggy creations. For example, the *Laced Pants* (page 110) use grommets to add interest to a side panel. If you like the *Denim Ballgown Skirt* (page 98) and want to make extreme bell-bottoms instead, just open up the side seams as you would for that skirt and attach extra denim or other fabric. Or, if you like the *Dual-Fabric Skirt* (page 96), cut off a pair of corduroys at the knee and add wild printed flannel to take winter-weight pants to a new level. The fun and funky projects shown in this chapter are really just a few of the many ways you can transform literally any pair of pants into something that's uniquely you.

LACED PANTS

Open up the side of a pair of pants and add contrasting colors or textures plus grommeted lacing. It's a fun way to add not only a new look to your pants but also some extra "give." Try this on the Perfect Pair of Pants in your closet or at the thrift store that are just slightly too tight in the waist or thighs. (Hey, it's faster than dieting!)

MATERIALS

PAIR OF PANTS THAT FIT YOU

½–1 YARD (46CM–91CM) CONTRASTING FABRIC

GROMMETS

RIBBON OR CORD (ENOUGH FOR LACING)

THREAD

GROMMET SETTER

HAMMER (OPTIONAL)

LEATHER PUNCH (OPTIONAL)

MEASURING TAPE

SCISSORS

1 RIP SEAMS OPEN

Use a seam ripper to rip both side seams open as far up from the bottom as you'd like to grommet, taking care to make the slits the same length on both sides. The pants shown were grommeted up their entire length, but if you prefer, you can go just to the knee or even just a little above the ankle.

2 CUT CONTRASTING STRIPS

Cut four strips of your contrasting fabric at least 3" (8cm) wide and the length of the slits plus 1" (3cm). This makes one strip for each side of each slit.

3 FOLD AND IRON STRIPS

Fold each strip in half lengthwise, wrong sides together, and iron flat. Fold under ¾" (19mm) to the wrong side on all four edges of each strip, and iron flat. This will keep the raw edges tucked under when you sew the pieces down to the pants.

DARE TO BE BRIGHT

The more color and texture the better. Try a brightly colored solid or print fabric with a pair of plain black pants, silk brocade on corduroy pants, heavily embroidered yardage (widely available at fabric stores in the "ethnic prints" section) with jeans. Maximum contrast makes this look work.

4 ATTACH THE STRIPS

Wrap the strips around the raw edges of the slits and pin into place. Sew the strip down, stitching ½" (13mm) away from its edge. Depending on the fabric's weight and your machine's capabilities, you may need to sew the bottom and top edges down by hand if they're too thick.

5 ADD GROMMETS

Mark where the grommets will go, matching pairs on both side of the slits, with a grommet's width of space between each, vertically. Punch holes in the fabric after you've marked each grommet's location and set the grommets according to your grommet setter's directions. If you want the pants completely closed, grommet all the way down to the bottom. For a flared look (as shown), stop at about midcalf.

6 ADD LACING

Lace the sides up and tie in a bow.

1¢ SALE
GUARANTEED
10 YEARS

PIECED PANTS

MATERIALS

SEVERAL PAIRS OF
PANTS (PAIRS WITH
SIMILAR LEG WIDTHS
WILL BE EASIEST TO
WORK WITH)

THREAD

MEASURING TAPE
OR RULER

SCISSORS

STRAIGHT PINS

SEWING MACHINE

These pants are another example of "more is more" (our version of "less is more"). For the most visual impact, add as many different fabric types as you can, i.e. not just denim, not just corduroy, not just velvet. These pants look best with wildly contrasting colors, prints and textures. Or you could play it safe and just use different colors of jeans—but where's the fun in that?

1 MEASURE AND CUT PANTS

Measure the inseam from crotch to hem of a well-fitting pair of pants. Keep this measurement handy. Cut the top pair of pants (which should fit you well in the waist) to shorts length. Cut tubes from the legs of your other pairs of pants. These tubes should be cut the length you want them in the finished pants, plus 1" (3cm) for seam allowances. Keep the legs of one pair intact below the knees (you'll use these for the bottom of your pieced pants).

2 PIN THE TUBES TOGETHER

Pin all of the tubes together in your preferred order, with the tubes inside out and right sides of the fabric touching. Pin where the seam lines will be, ½" (13mm) from the raw edges.

You may need to add or trim tubes to get the proper length. The fabric patterns on each side don't have to match, but you'll probably want the overall length of the legs to. If any of tubes are slightly wider than the others, you'll need to take their side seams in a little so they'll match the others.

3 SEW PANTS

Sew the fabric tubes together, with ½" (13mm) seam allowances. We've made the leg as one piece first, because sometimes it's easier (depending on your fabrics and machine) to connect the multiple-tubed, already-sewn lower portion of the leg to the upper shorts all at once than it is add each additional piece as you go along. It also makes it easier to check that both legs match (if you want them to).

TRIMMED PANTS

Sometimes you want a simple project: just a little pick-me-up, an extra bit of wardrobe "oomph!" This is that project. You'll probably spend longer picking out the trim than you will actually sewing it on! You can also use this approach on denim jackets—the sleeves look really cool when cut to three-quarter length and embellished with trim.

MATERIALS

PAIR OF PANTS

1–1½ YARDS (1–1½M) LACE OR OTHER TRIM

THREAD

MEASURING TAPE OR RULER

SCISSORS

STRAIGHT PINS

SEWING MACHINE

1 CUT PANTS (OPTIONAL) AND PIN TRIM

Cut your pants off at your preferred length, unless they're already the length you want. Capri-length pants look good trimmed this way. Pin the trim in place.

2 SEW TRIM

Zigzag stitch the trim to the front of your pants, then to the back. Be careful not to stitch through both sides of the pants as you go! With lace or openwork trim such as this, use a slightly smaller stitch width than you might usually use to make sure you're catching as many of the threads in the lace as you can.

SIDE SEAM STYLE

For a really cool "swishy" look, try attaching fringe to the side seams of your jeans, or run a line of velvet ribbon up the seams of black pants. The possibilities are endless.

117

ACCESSORIES

Scarves, bags, boots—accessories are the playful, fun pieces that can transform even the plainest outfit into something amazing. And when your favorite accessories are altered and reinvented creations of your own, they become twice the fun. Our *Dangerous Cherry Handbag* (page 126) introduces yet another clever way to repurpose that old closet staple: worn jeans. The unique *Soluble Scarf* (page 120) transforms ordinary scraps of fabric into a fabulous cosy complement to your favorite sweater or jacket. And the three very different variations of our *Tie Store Explosion Collars* (page 132) will have your mind spinning at all the creative possibilities.

SOLUBLE SCARF

This is just like making a sandwich, except you're using dissolvable interfacing for the bread and scraps of yarn and fabric for the filling. After you make the basic piece, you can embroider the scarf with yarn or embroidery floss, add beads, or wear as is! Depending on what materials you layer in the center, this scarf can be very thick, woolly and fluffy, or it can be a thin, summery piece.

MATERIALS

ASSORTED FABRIC AND YARN SCRAPS, WOOL FIBER AND LEFT-OVER WOOL SWEATER BITS

WATER-SOLUBLE STABILIZER (WE USED SULKY BRAND SOLVY, WHICH COMES IN A ROLL, LIKE PLASTIC WRAP.)

MATCHING AND CONTRASTING THREADS

SCISSORS

STRAIGHT PINS (LOTS OF THEM!)

YARN NEEDLE (OPTIONAL)

CLOTHES DRYER

SEWING MACHINE

1 ARRANGE SCRAPS ON STABILIZER

Spread out a layer of water-soluble stabilizer the length you'd like the finished scarf to be. Arrange your fabric and yarn scraps on top until the stabilizer is completely covered. Overlap the pieces generously; this will help them stay together once the stabilizer is dissolved and only stitches are holding them together. Place another layer of stabilizer on top.

2 PIN EVERYTHING TOGETHER

You'll want to put many pins around the outer edges and many more inside, closely spaced, to keep everything from falling out as you sew.

3 SEW EVERYTHING TOGETHER

Sew over the fiber "sandwich" with lots of stitching. You can stitch randomly, with a zigzag, in tight squares or in any configuration, using as many colors as you like. Just be sure to cover the entire piece with more stitches than you think you would possibly ever need, because they're all that holds the scraps together. Watch out for pins while you're stitching.

4 SOAK AND DRY SCARF

Soak your scarf in water. The stabilizer will dissolve and you'll be left with a funky scarf! Rinse thoroughly, squeeze out the excess water, and hang to drip dry. When the scarf is very nearly dry, put it in the dryer for 10 minutes. This will tighten any wool pieces and fling loose bits off the scarf where you didn't stitch enough. Hold the scarf up and look for any unattractive holes or sections where the stitching has torn apart. Hand stitch them closed as needed, or leave loose for a wilder look.

lettuce knit

68½ nassau street · kensington market
toronto, ontario · m5t1m5
416-203-9970
www.lettuceknit.com
info@lettuceknit.com

supplies for the next generation of knitters

1¢ SALE
GUARANTEED
10 YEARS

SQUARE-BOTTOM BAG

Do you have a huge collection of giveaway bags from events? Shannon's got an entire wall of them in her studio filled with craft materials. This is for you. The problem with many tote bags is that they're sewn straight up the sides and don't have any room in the bottom to carry things. This project can easily fix that flaw! Not only does it teach you to sew a cool-looking new lining into your bag, but it squares off the bottom so you can tote all you want. No matter what fabrics you use—and the more, the merrier—these bags are fun to make and even more fun to carry.

MATERIALS

EXISTING UNLINED TOTE BAG

APPROXIMATELY 1–2 YARDS (1–2M) OF FABRIC FOR THE LINING

THREAD

MEASURING TAPE OR RULER

SCISSORS

STRAIGHT PINS

SEWING MACHINE

1 PREPARE LINING

To line the bag, fold your chosen lining fabric in half, wrong side facing out, and trim it to the same size as your bag plus 2" (5cm) on each side and 2" (5cm) on the top. (This is for the seam allowance and for folding over the top when stitching in the liner.) Iron the liner and the bag. Sew the sides of the lining closed and leave the top open.

2 ARRANGE LINING

Turn the bag inside out and grab the sides of a bottom corner. Pinch the corner open and flatten it (you'll be making a triangular point, as shown). Arrange the bottom of the lining so it comes to a point at the end of the side seam. Put the bag on top of the lining where the width of the bottom seam matches the width of the triangle in the lining.

123

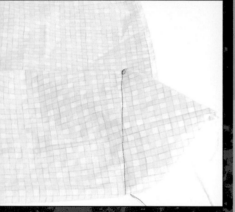

3 ADJUST BOTTOM WIDTH

To make the bag and its lining wider at the bottom, sew a new line of stitching on the outer bag farther in from the raw edge.

4 ADJUST LINING

Sew the lining straight across the bottom of the triangle at the same depth you chose for your tote bag in step 3 [in our example, where it measures 4" (10cm)]. Repeat on the other side, being sure to make the triangles the same size.

5 TRIM EXCESS FABRIC

You'll see the bottom is now a roomy rectangle instead of an envelope-style sleeve. You may trim off the excess triangle fabric past the line of stitching if you like.

6 SEW LINING IN PLACE

Insert the lining into the bag, wrong sides together, and match up the squared-off portions of the lining and outer bag. Pin them together from the outside so you won't sew the lining in too high. Along the top of the back, fold the lining to the inside of the bag and stitch in place. If you want to replace the straps, you can pin the new straps in place either between the lining and the bag, or on the inside over the lining.

A bottom view of the Square-Bottom Bag when filled

VARIATION: QUILTED BAG

For the variation shown here, I pinned a piece of quilt batting to the back of the Maker Faire logo with a scrap of fabric behind it. I quilted the logo by hand, stitching around the outside of the blue square and around the letters M and F.

DON'T STOP WITH THE LINING

Tote bags are prime candidates for reverse appliqué and other decorative techniques. What about a corduroy bag with a brightly colored lining showing through crochet cutouts (see page 61)? Or handles made of plastic tubing from the hardware store with coordinating fabric threaded inside?

DANGEROUS
CHERRY HANDBAG

You should always be on the lookout for unusual materials that could make their way into your designs. Chains suggest a certain Chanel-like quality (Chanel's couture jackets have a small gold chain sewn into the hem to ensure the jacket hangs properly, and their purses often feature chain handles). Of course, this handbag is a little tougher than your average socialite, hence its "dangerous" tag. These chains could take out a mugger if you heaved the purse in the right direction!

MATERIALS

BLACK JEANS

1 YARD (1M) CHERRY PRINT FABRIC (OR FABRIC OF YOUR CHOICE)

1 YARD (1M) METAL CHAIN (FROM A HARDWARE STORE)

PLASTIC NEEDLE-POINT CANVAS (PREFERRED) OR HEAVY CARDBOARD CUT TO FIT THE BOTTOM OF YOUR BAG (SEE STEP 6)

2 METAL KEY RING LOOPS (OPTIONAL)

PAPER GROCERY BAG

PENCIL

THREAD

MEASURING TAPE

SCISSORS

STRAIGHT PINS

SEWING MACHINE

1 CLIP INSEAM OPEN
Clip open the inseam of the jeans as shown on page 99. Be careful to cut only the stitches without nicking the fabric.

2 CLIP CROTCH SEAM
Clip through the crotch seam and keep going down the other inseam as shown on page 99.

3 CUT FABRIC NEXT TO FRONT CROTCH SEAM
Cut the fabric right next to the front crotch seam just past the curve as shown on page 100.

4 CUT FABRIC NEXT TO BACK CROTCH SEAM
Cut the fabric right next to the back crotch seam just past the curve as shown on page 100.

5 OVERLAP AND SEW
Overlap the 2 sides of the front crotch seam and sew them together, as shown on page 100. Repeat this for the back crotch seam.

DETERMINE BOTTOM PANEL MEASUREMENTS

To determine how big your bag's bottom should be, measure the bottom opening of your cut-off jeans [once you've sewn the crotch piece down flat, then subtract the total number of inches (or centimeters) you want the right and left side pieces to be. Divide the remaining number in half to find the length of the bottom panel. Say you have a 38" opening and you want 4" side panels. Subtract (4+4) from 38=30. Divide 30 by 2=15. Your bottom panel would thus measure 15" x 4". Cut 2 rectangles the size of the bag bottom, 1 from your lining fabric and 1 from the denim, then cut a piece of plastic needlepoint canvas or heavy cardboard to the same size.

6

SEW IN BOTTOM PANEL

Turn the bag body inside out and pin the denim piece you just cut to the bottom opening. Sew it closed with ½" (13mm) seam allowances. Turn the bag right side out. Insert the plastic needlepoint canvas inside the bag bottom.

7

CREATE LINING

Sew a lining the same size and shape as your bag. (You already have the correct size lining bottom rectangle from step 2. To make a rough pattern for the body itself, cut open the paper grocery bag so it lies flat and trace the bag's shape on the paper. Use this paper pattern to cut out 2 main pieces for the inner lining. Sew the bottom lining rectangle to these 2 pieces (with the wrong side of the fabric facing out) and insert into the bag.

8

SEW IN THE LINING

Turn the raw top edges of the lining under and pin into place. Stitch the lining to the top of the bag. Depending on your machine and the thickness of the pants used, you may want to do this by hand or use a denim needle.

9

ATTACH CHAIN

Loop the chain through the belt loops. Here, we used a metal key ring loop to attach either side of the chain to each other, but you could also open up a loop and close it around the other side directly. (Someone at the hardware store where you bought the chain should be able to help you with this.)

10

REMEMBER PLASTIC NEEDLEPOINT CANVAS?

Plastic needlepoint canvas is that stuff your childhood art teacher used to make acrylic-yarn-stitchery fridge magnets and the like. It's lightweight, yet sturdy and flexible. You can use a rectangular piece of it to keep the bottom of your bag flat and stiff

PAINTED COWBOY BOOTS

Home on the range just got a lot more colorful with these fun boots! This technique will work on cowboy boots, Doc Martens—any leather boot that's got some blank space to fill. If you have boots that have been scuffed up more times than they've been polished, you can cover all the bad spots and get a whole new look to boot.

MATERIALS

BOOTS

VARIOUS COLORS OF PAINT (OIL HOLDS UP NICELY BUT ACRYLIC WILL DO)

CLEAR VARNISH (OPTIONAL)

FINE-GRIT SANDPAPER (OPTIONAL)

PERMANENT MARKER (OPTIONAL)

PAINTBRUSHES

1 PREPARE SURFACE

If your boots are shiny and new, you'll want to roughen the surface a little to give the paint something to stick to firmly. Gently rub the boots in the areas you intend to paint with fine-grit sandpaper (a manicure block will also work in a pinch).

2 PLAN YOUR DESIGN

Lay out the design. If you're not comfortable painting free-hand, use a marker to lay out the basic design. Are you painting cowboy boots with a stitching pattern on the uppers? Use the stitching as a basis for your design, or doodle with the marker for paint-by-numbers fun later.

3 PAINT BOOTS

Paint the boots as desired. Can't paint? Can't even paint by number? Go for the Jackson Pollock look by filling your brush with paint, then flicking it at the boots (don't forget to put down newspapers first!).

4 SPRAY ON FINISH (OPTIONAL)

Spray the boots with clear varnish for a shiny finish and to preserve the paint.

TIE STORE
EXPLOSION COLLAR

These stand-alone collars made of ties (to be worn with a shirt, jacket or winter coat) resemble old-school fur collars—you know, the creepy ones lurking in thrift stores everywhere. It's a clever take on neckwear that's easy to make and looks great with Tie Skirts (see page 92) if you're going for a wild night out.

MATERIALS

ASSORTMENT OF NECKTIES

HOOK AND EYE (OPTIONAL)

TAILOR'S CHALK

THREAD

MEASURING TAPE OR RULER

SCISSORS

STRAIGHT PINS

SEWING MACHINE OR NEEDLE

1 CREATE THE BASE
Two ties make up the base that goes around your neck. Drape the two ties around your neck, with the wide part of each tie in front. Ask a sewing buddy to hold the two ties together at the back of your neck while you adjust them in front so they come together where you want them. Ask your friend to mark the ties where they come together behind your neck. Lay the ties out straight and flat, overlapping where your friend marked them. Sew the ties and trim off the excess. This overlapped seam will be covered with looped ties very shortly.

2 BEGIN LAYING OUT TIES
Lay out four ties side by side with their points aligned and their edges overlapping slightly. Pin the ties together.

3 MEASURE AND MARK
Mark a line 8" (20cm) from the points.

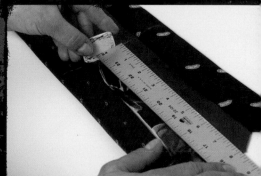

4 SEW TIES TOGETHER
Sew the ties together along the marked line.

5 TRIM EXCESS
Mark another line 30" (76cm) from the tips of the ties and trim off the excess.

133

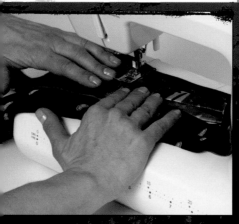

6 MARK AND FOLD

On the backs of the ties, mark a another line 8" (20cm) from the tips. Fold the cut ends over to the wrong side and pin the cut edges to the marked line.

7 SEW LOOPS

Stitch the first loops into place.

8 FOLD AND PIN

Fold the ties over to the right side and pin them so the folds are about 4" (10cm) from the tips of the ties. Mark a line about 5" (13cm) from the folds and sew down the loops on the marked line.

9 FOLD AGAIN

Fold the ties over again with the folds about 4" (10cm) from the first row of folds and pin the loops in place. Mark a line about 4" (10cm) from the second set of loops and stitch on the marked line.

10 SEW LOOPS TO BASE

Attach the loops to your base ties by sewing across the row of stitching you sewed in step 9. If you're working with particularly delicate fabrics or if your sewing machine has a tough time handling thick fabrics, you may want to stitch the looped ties down to the base by hand. Repeat from step 1, adding looped ties to the two foundation ties until you get to the other end.

VARIATION: FLAT-TIE COLLAR

For the flat collar, create the base (two ties sewn together; see step 1), then trim the ties that will make up the points as short as you'd like them to be. (This is, by the way, a great way to use up ends from making tie skirts.) Tucking the cut ends under, stitch the ties into place on the base.

If you stitch them down with only one straight line, the ties will be "floppier" and more inclined to move. Don't like that? Add a few more lines of stitching parallel to the first to keep them from moving around on the base.

VARIATION: QUEEN LIZ COLLAR

This scarf-style collar is meant to evoke the high neck pieces of Queen Elizabeth I and her court and can be as sedate or as wild as you like. This variation is a snap if you have basic knitting knowledge. Start collecting scraps from other projects (or laundry felting accidents) in the summer and you'll have more than enough to make yours by the time the first snow falls. To keep the collar fastened snugly in the dead of winter, you can stitch it down to your coat, attach a snap closure or use a vintage button and buttonhole, as we did.

STEP 1 | FELT SWEATER

Throw your wool sweater into your washing machine with a hot wash and cold rinse until it shrinks. (Some sweaters, particularly light-colored ones or wool blends, may take more than one cycle to shrink appropriately; keep going until the fabric is solid and you cannot see the individual stitches.) Spin the excess water out of the sweater and place it on a flat surface to dry.

STEP 2 | DETERMINE MEASUREMENTS

To determine your size, put on the coat you plan to wear the collar with and wrap the measuring tape around your neck like a necklace, ending at the top of your collar bone or the second button from the top of your coat. Record this measurement. Knit a gauge swatch and measure the number of stitches per 4" (10cm), then divide by 4 to get the average stitches per inch (centimeter). Multiply the stitches per inch by the collar measurement you took to determine the number of stitches you will need to cast on. The sample was knit in seed stitch: knit 1, purl 1 all the way across the row then purl the knits and knit the purls on the way back across. You can use any reversible knit/purl pattern, or even a simple garter stitch (knit across all rows).

STEP 3 | MAKE COLLAR FOUNDATION PIECE

Cast on the number of stitches determined by your measurement, working loosely to create a stretchy edge for the outside of your collar. For this collar, we cast on 125 stitches. Work in your pattern stitch until the piece measures 2" (5cm), and create a buttonhole if desired. Bind off all stitches firmly in pattern. The loose cast-on edge and firm bind off will cause the knit piece to curve slightly, helping the collar rest nicely around your neck. This knitted strip will be the foundation for your felted loops.

MATERIALS

WOOL SWEATER

APPROXIMATELY 100 YARDS (91M) WORSTED-WEIGHT WOOL YARN (SHOWN HERE: CASCADE 220, COLOR 4002)

BUTTON OR OTHER CLOSURE (OPTIONAL)

MASKING TAPE

THREAD

KNITTING NEEDLES, STRAIGHT OR CIRCULAR, U.S. SIZE #10 (6MM)

MEASURING TAPE

ROTARY CUTTER OR SCISSORS

SEWING NEEDLE

STRAIGHT PINS

STRAIGHTEDGE

WASHING MACHINE (FOR FELTING)

STEP 4 | CUT UP SWEATER

Cut apart your sweater as follows: Take the arms off at the armhole seam and leave them intact. Open up the body of the sweater by slicing open 1 shoulder and 1 side seam. Cut the body of the sweater into 30–40 strips of felt, from ½"–1" (13mm–25mm) wide and at least 6" (15cm) long. An easy way to cut these strips is to lay a straightedge on top of the felted material and cut along it with a rotary cutter. The more irregular the pieces are in length and width, the wilder the finished collar will look.

STEP 5 | CUT MASKING TAPE

Carefully place a strip of masking tape about 1 yard (1m) long sticky side up on your work surface. You may want to tape the ends down to the table to keep it from moving.

STEP 6 | MAKE LOOPS

Create loops by folding each felt strip in half, then arrange them, with the longest loops at the center, along the piece of masking tape. The final ½" (13mm) of each felt strip should extend past the tape, and each loop should just touch its neighbor. By arranging it so that all of the biggest loops are in the center of the piece, you create a collar that's fuller in the back and smaller in the front. Optional: To make the loops stand up higher, stick the left edge of the loop down, then put a half-twist in the loop before aligning the right end of the loop in place. This not only makes the loops more dimensional, but it also keeps everything in one layer so your sewing machine doesn't have to stitch through layers of thick felt.

STEP 7 | MAKE MORE LOOPS

Repeat steps 5–6 to make a second line of loops adhered to masking tape. (The rows of loops need to be sewn together edge to edge before you sew them onto the collar. Masking tape is simpler to use than pins. You can tear it off without harming the stitches after sewing the felted loops together in their continuous strip.

STEP 8 | SEW LOOPS

Sew across the middle of the masking tape attaching your loop strips with your machine and then remove the masking tape.

STEP 9 | CUT UP SLEEVES

Make loops out of the sweater sleeves by laying each sleeve flat so that the seam is on the bottom edge. Make cuts about ½"–1" (13mm–25mm) apart, beginning at the top edge of each flattened sleeve and stopping 1" (3cm) from the bottom. These loops are already attached in one continuous strip because of the sleeve seam, so the entire strip can be sewn directly onto the foundation piece.

STEP 10 | SEW LOOPS TO FOUNDATION PIECE

To assemble the collar, center the first strip of loops on the cast-on edge of the knitted foundation piece (which will be the outside edge when worn) and pin the strip in place. Stitch this strip down. Next, position the second strip ½" (13mm) from the first, moving toward the front edge of the foundation piece. Sew this strip in place. The sliced sleeves should be positioned on the front edge of the foundation with the cuffs at the ends of the collar and the wide ends (formerly the sleeve shoulders) at the center. Once this is assembled, you can either sew it directly onto your coat if you want it to be permanently attached, or put a button or other fastener on the front edges so you can take it on and off.

THE GUIDE

Our favorite resources for inspiration, materials and instruction.

Magazines

ADORN
www.adornmag.com

BELLE ARMOIRE
www.bellearmoire.com

CRAFT
www.craftzine.com

CROCHET TODAY
www.crochettoday.com

CUTTING EDGE
www.cuttingedgemag.com

INTERWEAVE CROCHET
www.interweavecrochet.com

KNITSCENE
www.knitscene.com

Materials

C. JENKINS NECKTIE & CHEMICAL COMPANY
www.cjenkinscompany.com
Bubble Jet Set and Bubble Jet Rinse

DHARMA TRADING COMPANY
www.dharmatrading.com
ink-jet transfer paper

EARTHENWOOD STUDIO
www.earthenwoodstudio.com
custom buttons

REPRODEPOT
www.reprodepot.com
fabric, buttons, embellishments, you name it

Web Sites

WWW.ALTERNATIONBOOK.COM

WWW.ARTOFXAN.COM

WWW.KNITGRRL.COM

WWW.CROCHETME.COM

WWW.CRAFTSTER.ORG

WWW.BAZAARBIZARRE.ORG

WWW.RENEGADECRAFT.COM

WWW.WHIPUP.NET

SUBLIME STITCHING
www.sublimestitching.com
iron-on transfer patterns

SULKY OF AMERICA
www.sulky.com
iron-on transfer pens,
Solvy water-soluble stabilizer

Books

LEARN TO KNIT

Knitgrrl. Learn to Knit with 15 Fun and Funky Patterns, Shannon Okey (Watson-Guptill Publications, 2005)

Knitgrrl 2: Learn to Knit with 16 All-New Patterns, Shannon Okey (Watson-Guptill Publications, 2006)

Knitting in Plain English, Maggie Righetti (St. Martin's Griffin, 2007)

Knitting Rules! The Yarn Harlot's Bag of Knitting Tricks, Stephanie Pearl-McPhee (Storey Publishing, 2006)

Stitch 'n Bitch: The Knitter's Handbook, Debbie Stoller (Workman Publications, 2003)

LEARN TO CROCHET

Crochet Style: Chic and Sexy Accessories, Shannon Okey (Creative Homeowner, 2006)

Get Hooked: Simple Steps to Crochet Cool Stuff, Kim Werker (Watson-Guptill Publications, 2006)

Teach Yourself Visually: Crocheting, Kim Werker and Cecily Keim (Wiley, 2006)

LEARN TO FELT

Felt Frenzy: 26 Projects for All Forms of Felting, Shannon Okey and Heather Brack (Interweave Press, 2007)

Felted Knits, Beverly Galeskas (Interweave Press, 2003)

LEARN MORE ABOUT SEWING AND ALTERING CLOTHING

The Art of Fabric Collage: An Easy Introduction to Creative Sewing, Rosemary Eichorn (Taunton Press, 2003)

The Art of Manipulating Fabric, Colette Wolff (Chilton Book Company, 1996)

Generation T: 108 Ways to Transform a T-Shirt, Megan Nicolay (Workman Publications, 2006)

Second-Time Cool: The Art of Chopping Up a Sweater, Anna-Stina Linden Ivarsson, Katarina Brieditis and Katarina Evans (Annick Press, 2005)

Tease: 50 Inspired T-shirt Transformations by Superstars of Art, Craft and Design, Sarah Sockit (Perigee, 2006)

GET INSPIRED!

Bazaar Bizarre: Not Your Granny's Crafts, Greg Der Ananian (Viking Studio, 2005)

Super Crafty: Over 75 Amazing How-To Projects, Susan Beal, Torie Nguyen, Rachel O'Rourke and Cathy Pitters (Sasquatch Books, 2005)

PLUS-SIZE HELP

Big Girl Knits: 25 Big, Bold Projects Shaped for Real Women with Real Curves, Jillian Moreno and Amy R. Singer (Potter Craft, 2006)

ALSO BY SHANNON OKEY

Just Gifts: Favorite Patterns to Knit and Crochet (Potter Craft, 2007)
Just Socks: Favorite Patterns to Knit and Crochet (Potter Craft, 2007)
Spin to Knit: The Knitter's Guide to Making Yarn (Interweave Press, 2006)
The Pillow Book (Chronicle Books, 2008)

INDEX

CUSTOMIZE YOUR CREATIVE STYLE WITH THESE OTHER GREAT TITLES FROM F+W PUBLICATIONS.

Plush You!
Kristen Rask

This showcase of 100 plush toys, many with patterns and instructions, will inspire you to join in the DIY toy phenomenon. The wildly popular *Plush You!* show is now available in book form, featuring a gallery of plushies from around the world as well as 15 step-by-step plush projects. Stuffed space creatures and lovable monsters, along with the occasional cut of beef and other squeezable subjects, make this an irresistibly hip book you just want to hug.

ISBN-10: 1-58180-996-4
ISBN-13: 978-1-58180-996-1
paperback with flaps, 144 pages, Z0951

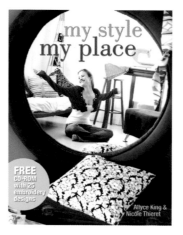

My Style My Place
Allyce King and Nicole Thieret

This book for the DIY segment of the Generation Y crowd empowers youthful sewers to create projects for their wardrobes and their homes to fit their personalities. With easy-to-follow instructions for 20 quick sewing and embroidery projects, *My Style My Place* encourages creativity and individuality while introducing readers to new avenues for expressing themselves through their craft.

ISBN-10: 0-89689-538-6
ISBN-13: 978-0-89689-538-6
paperback, 128 pages, Z0935

DomiKNITrix
Jennifer Stafford

Whip your knitting into shape with this no-nonsense, comprehensive guide to essential knitting operations and finishing techniques, including step-by-step instructions for all the basic stitches used in the book. Then get your hands dirty with more than 20 spicy projects to satisfy any knitting appetite. Projects range from smaller items like naughty candy heart pillows and a mohawk hat to more complicated pieces like the L'il Red Riding Hoodie. Just let the *DomiKNITrix* show you how it's done.

ISBN-10: 1-58180-853-4
ISBN-13: 978-1-58180-853-7
flexibind, 256 pages, Z0171

These and other fine North Light Books are available at your local craft or scrapbook store, bookstore or from online suppliers.